Beauty and the Pig

A Study of Godly Beauty

by Pam Forster

Doorposts

5905 SW Lookingglass Drive, Gaston, OR 97119

ISBN 978-1-891206-19-1

Doorposts

5905 SW Lookingglass Drive, Gaston, OR 97119

"Of beauty vain, or virtue void,
What art thou in the sight of God?
A slave to every base desire,
A creature wallowing in the mire.
Go, gaudy pageant of a day,
Thy folly, with thy face display;
Set all thy charms and graces out,
And shew—the Jewel in thy snout!"

From John Wesley's
Explanatory Notes on the Whole Bible

This book of studies is dedicated
to the memory of

Johanna Driesner,

a beautiful, godly woman,
who placed before me,
from my earliest memories,
an inspiring and winsome example
of quiet rest in her Savior.

Table of Contents

Introduction

Our Purpose:

The purpose of this collection of studies is two-fold:

First, we want our own children, and others, to understand the difference between outward beauty and true inner beauty. What does the Bible say about beauty? What does it say about the attitudes that God values in a young woman's heart? What actions are characteristic in the life of a truly beautiful woman? What attitudes and actions detract from, or even render disgusting, a woman's physical beauty?

Second, we want our children, and others, to learn to mine for the riches that are hidden in God's Word. We want them to be obedient students of God's Word. Our sons will grow to be leaders in their homes, churches, and community. They need to know how to study God's Word. Our daughters will be sources of counsel and encouragement to their husbands. They need to know what God's Word says. God reveals Himself and His will through His Word. In Scripture, He has given us commands, principles, examples, guidance, and comfort.

2 Timothy 3:16 and 17 tells us that, "All scripture is given by inspiration of God, and is profitable for doctrine, for reproof, for correction, for instruction in righteousness: that the man of God may be perfect, thoroughly furnished unto all good works." God's Word tells us how to live and how to please God. We learn much from God-given pastors and teachers; we also learn from direct interaction with His Word.

Besides consistent daily reading of Scripture, we should also slow down and *study* God's Word. Personal Bible study brings the Bible to life. The depths of the riches of God's Word are unfathomable. It is very exciting to understand this in a new way as we do our own digging into Scripture.

While engaging in personal Bible study, we are, however, responsible to study what God actually says, not what we *think* God says. We must always study prayerfully, with the guidance of the Holy Spirit. In addition, many practices and resources will aid us in careful, responsible study. The following are examples of methods that young ladies can easily employ while studying the Bible:

* Studying the original Hebrew or Greek words as they are used throughout Scripture
* Comparing one passage of Scripture with another
* Observing repeated words and themes in a passage
* Outlining the content of the passage
* Gathering all of Scripture's words about a particular topic
* Studying the lives of people in the Bible, and noting how their attitudes and actions portray the truths of Scripture

While studying godly beauty in **Beauty and the Pig**, young ladies will also learn the fundamentals of several Bible study methods. They will learn how to use a concordance, how to find the original word used in a passage and how it is used in other passages, how to study a specific topic, how to use marginal study notes, how to study a verse, passage, or entire chapter or book of the Bible, and how to perform a character study.

In addition, each study concludes with suggestions for further study. Besides the ten expanded studies that are included in this book, 32 other related studies are also suggested. Young ladies can continue to develop their study skills as they use the Bible study methods they have learned to pursue these additional study topics. This book provides study material that can keep young ladies busy studying for more than a year!

Recommended Materials:

To fully benefit from these studies, you will need **Nave's Topical Bible** and **Strong's Exhaustive Concordance of the Bible**. Both are study tools that your family will use over and over. When our children leave home to establish their own households, we will make sure their libraries include both of these books.

These are easily obtainable. Any Christian bookstore or online Christian book supplier sells them. You may be able to borrow the books to do these studies if you are unsure about the investment, but after you see their value you will probably want to buy them.

Computer software is also available that includes both **Nave's Topical Bible** and **Strong's Exhaustive Concordance**. For the purpose of these studies, hard-copy book versions will be easier to use.

Many may prefer to study in a translation other than the King James Version of the Bible. To simplify the learning process, we have used only the King James Version. All lessons that explain the use of study tools will be referring to versions that are keyed to the King James Version.

However, concordances can be purchased for other translations. In your own further study, you may choose to use tools that are designed to use with your preferred translation.

Recommended age levels:

Because we designed these studies with our own daughters in mind, we know that they are appropriate for girls from nine years of age and older. Younger girls, working with a parent or older sister, could also benefit from the studies.

Study No. 3, "Beauty and the Pit," includes questions that are more appropriate for girls who have entered puberty. You may choose to skip over those questions, or simply save the entire study to complete when your young daughter is older.

For families with boys:

Consider completing these studies with the young men in your family. They need to know about true beauty! Many of the passages that describe godly beauty, including Proverbs 11:22, about the beautiful woman without discretion, were addressed to young men, not ladies! Studies can easily be adapted for the benefit of young men. For study questions that are marked with a star (✪), you will find alternate application questions on pages 101-106. These are designed to address the needs and goals of young men.

    i.   Proverbs 26:16 (reason)

_____

    j.   Jonah 3:7 (decree)

_____

8. Review your notes. What common factors do you see in how the word "taam" is used?

_____

_____

_____

9. Read the following definition of **discretion** as it is defined in Noah Webster's 1828 **American Dictionary of the English Language**:

> Prudence, or knowledge and prudence; that discernment which enables a person to judge critically of what is correct and proper, united with caution; nice discernment and judgment; directed by circumspection, and primarily regarding one's own conduct.

How does this definition apply to the word **discretion** as it is used in Proverbs 11:22?

_____

_____

_____

10. Read Webster's definition of **taste**.

> To perceive by means of the tongue; to have a certain sensation in consequence of something applied to the tongue, the organ of taste; as, to taste bread; to taste wine; to taste a sweet or an acid.

How does this definition apply to the word **discretion** as used in Proverbs 11:22?

_____

_____

_____

11. Perform the following experiments:

    a.   Ask a family member, without allowing you to watch, to put salt in one spoon and sugar in another spoon. Imagine that you are about to have a bowl of oatmeal and would like to sweeten it a bit. Which spoonful will you add to your cereal? What is the most reliable way to decide which spoonful you should pour onto your cereal?

_____

b. Bake a loaf of bread for your family's dinner. Follow any reliable recipe, preferably one that your family has enjoyed before. **Leave the salt out of the bread.** Before the butter is passed around, ask family members to taste your bread. Can they tell that anything is missing? How can they tell? (To make your bread more enjoyable for the rest of the meal, pass the saltshaker around!)

_____

c. Cut a small slice of onion and a small piece of apple. Wearing a blindfold and pinching your nose closed, have someone else feed you the onion first, and then the apple. Can you tell which is which? What happens if you unplug your nose?

_____

_____

_____

12. Do your observations from the experiments help you better understand the meaning of "taam?" How can a beautiful woman be "without taste" or "without discretion?"

_____

_____

_____

_____

_____

13. Review all your notes from this study; then write your own paraphrase of Proverbs 11:22. Write the verse in a way that will demonstrate your understanding of **discretion**.

_____

_____

_____

_____

_____

14. As we learned in Question 3, the Bible uses a word for **beautiful** that means "to be bright." Read Ecclesiastes 8:1. What does it say about wisdom and physical beauty?

_____

_____

_____

15. ★ Read Proverbs 1:1-9. What is the purpose of the Book of Proverbs? How does this relate to the discretion that young ladies should possess?

_____

_____

_____

16. Outline a specific plan that will help you grow in your ability to make wise judgments. How will you know how to behave in a proper way? How will you choose the correct way to respond to different situations throughout the day? Will you choose to read God's Word for a specific amount of time each day? Will you study a particular topic in the Bible that could lead you to greater wisdom? Will you ask your parents for more guidance? Will you listen to authorities more carefully and obey them more diligently? Share your plan with someone that will help hold you accountable.

_____

_____

_____

_____

_____

_____

For Further Study:

- Look up the word **discretion** in **Strong's Exhaustive Concordance.** Using the method outlined in Study No. 4, "Beauty and the Drip," find the word that is No. 4209 in Strong's Hebrew dictionary. Study the verses that use this word. How do they relate to Proverbs 11:22?

- Study the story of Rebekah in Genesis 24. Rebekah was a beautiful woman (Genesis 29:17) whose actions reflected her discreet and humble spirit. She was also given the same kind of gold ring that the pig in Proverbs 11:22 wears. What can you learn about beauty and discretion from Rebekah's example?

Study No. 2
Beauty and the Pig

*"As a jewel of gold in a swine's snout,
so is a fair woman which is without discretion."*
(Proverbs 11:22)

What does the Bible say about pigs? How are gold rings like beautiful women, and how are gold rings in pigs' snouts like beautiful women without discretion? To better understand the meaning of Proverbs 11:22, we need to do some more studying.

You will need a concordance for this type of study. If you have an exhaustive concordance, such as **Strong's Exhaustive Concordance**, you will be using it throughout this book of studies. If you have a concordance in the back of your Bible, it may list some of the verses we are seeking, but will not list them all.

Pigs in the Bible

1. If you have access to **Strong's Exhaustive Concordance,** use it to look up the word **swine**. The words in the concordance are listed in alphabetical order. Under the word swine, you will see a listing that looks like the one below.

Le	11: 7	the *s*, though he divide the hoof	2386
De	14: 8	the *s*, because he divideth the hoof	"
M't	7: 6	neither cast ye…pearls before *s*	*5519*
	8: 30	them an herd of many *s* feeding	"
	31	us to go away into the herd of *s*,	"
	32	out, they went into the herd of *s*	"
	32	whole herd of *s* feeding	"
M'r	5: 11	a great herd of *s* feeding.	"
	12	Send us into the *s* that we may	"
	13	went out, and entered into the *s* :	"
	14	they that fed the *s* fled, and told *	"
	16	the devil, and also concerning the *s* .	"
Lu	8: 32	an herd of many *s* feeding on the	"
	33	of the man, and entered into the *s*	"
	15: 15	he sent him into his fields to feed *s*	"
	16	with the husks that the *s* did eat:	"

The abbreviation and numbers at the beginning of each line indicate the reference of each verse in which the word **swine** is used. The words in the center of each line quote the portion of the verse that contains the word **swine**. The "s" in each quote stands for the word **swine**. If you are unfamiliar with standard abbreviations for the books of the Bible, refer to the list of abbreviations provided at the beginning of the concordance.

2. What is the first reference listed? _____

3. Read this verse. What does it say about swine?

    _____

    _____

4. To fully understand this verse, you should also read the verses that precede it in the chapter, and the verses that follow it. These verses are called the **context**.

    If you were to overhear only one sentence in a conversation between two people, you might very well misunderstand what they were talking about. In the same way, if you only read one Bible verse by itself, out of its context, you may misunderstand what the passage is actually saying. Read the other verses around this verse. Then note anything else you have learned about swine from the passage.

    _____

    _____

    _____

5. Look again at the concordance listing. What is the next verse that is listed?

    _____

6. Read this verse and its context. What does it say about swine?

    _____

    _____

    _____

7. What is the third verse shown in the concordance listing?

    _____

8. Read this verse and note what it says about swine. (Continue to examine the context of each verse you look up as you do this study.)

    _____

    _____

    _____

9. What is the fourth verse listed in the concordance listing? Note that this listing does not include an abbreviated name of a book of the Bible. This means that the verse is found in the same book of the Bible as the previous listing. The previous verse was found in Matthew, so this next verse is also found in Matthew.

    _____

10. Read this verse and note what it says about swine.

_____

_____

_____

11. What is the next verse listed in the concordance? Following the same principle that was explained in Question 9, this listing does not show the book of the Bible or the chapter of the Bible. This means the verse is also in the same chapter as the previous verse. It is found in Matthew 8.

_____

12. Notice the following two listings in the concordance entry. Both of these are also from Matthew 8. Read the entire account given in Matthew 8, and note what you learn about swine.

_____

_____

_____

13. Look at the next 5 listings in the concordance entry. What book and chapter are they in?

_____

14. Read the verse quotations that are included with these references. What do you notice? The Gospel of Mark also includes an account of the story you read in Matthew. Read this passage and record anything new you notice in this passage.

_____

_____

_____

15. What do you notice about the references from the Gospel of Luke?

_____

16. Read this passage and record any new observations.

_____

_____

17. Now that you have learned how to use the concordance and read its listings, look up the word **swine's** in your concordance. List the references for verses that include this word.

_____

18. Read each of these verses, with their context, and record your observations below.

_____

_____

_____

_____

_____

_____

_____

_____

19. Another word used in Scripture for a pig is the word **boar**. Locate this word in your concordance. List the reference of the verse that includes this word.

_____

20. Read the verse and record your observations.

_____

_____

_____

21. One more word that the King James Bible uses for the pig is **sow**. Look this word up in your concordance, record the verse's reference, and note your observations below.

_____

_____

_____

22. Review the notes you have taken on all the verses that speak of pigs. Summarize your findings. What does the Bible say about pigs?

_____

_____

_____

_____

_____

_____

Gold in the Bible

23. Now that we know what the Bible says about pigs, lets learn more about gold. How is gold used in the Bible? What kinds of items were made of gold?

Using your concordance again, study the words **gold** and **golden**. There are many, many references to gold in the Bible. You won't be able to study every verse, and you won't need to in order to see many of the uses of gold. We're simply trying to get a **general** idea of how gold was used in Bible times. Skim through the concordance's brief excerpts from each verse. Many of these will be enough to tell you how the gold is being used.

Many times you will see a series of verses all taken from the same chapter of a book, indicating a longer passage that mentions gold being used for a specific purpose. Read enough of each of these chapters to see how the gold is being used. For instance, there are many verses listed from the book of Exodus. Examination of the verse excerpts will help you see that the gold is being used in the construction of the tabernacle and in crafting the articles in the tabernacle. Simply note this general observation.

List all your observations below.

_____

_____

_____

_____

_____

_____

_____

_____

_____

24. Review your observations about gold and summarize what you have found. What general categories of things were made with gold? What did gold symbolize?

_____

_____

_____

25. Combining your notes about pigs from Question 22 with your notes about gold in Question 24, how appropriate is a gold ring in a pig's nose? Why?

_____

_____

_____

26. In Study No. 1, "Beauty and the Word," we learned about earrings (or nose rings), beauty, and discretion. In this study we have learned about pigs and gold in the Bible.

In the chart, "The Pig and the Fool," on page 17, we will compare a gold ring in a pig's snout with a beautiful woman who has no discretion. How are the pig and the woman alike? Read the descriptions and verses indicated on the chart, and note, in the right hand column, how each relates to the beautiful woman without discretion.

After completing the chart, summarize your observations.

_____

_____

_____

27. The chart on page 18 will help you compare the traits that pigs and foolish women share. The top half of the chart examines Biblical passages about pigs and compares those with Scripture's description of the fool.

The lower portion of the chart deals with commonly recognized characteristics of pigs, and compares those with the Bible's description of the fool.

After completing the chart, summarize your observations.

_____

_____

_____

_____

_____

28. Review what you have learned in this study, and write a brief summary below. How is a beautiful woman without discretion like a gold ring in a pig's snout?

_____

_____

_____

29. ★ Examine your own life. Are there ways in which you are behaving like a pig? In what ways are you demonstrating a lack of discretion? List specific areas in which you need to change, share this list with your parents, pray for God's help, and commit to actions that will help you grow in wisdom.

_____

_____

_____

_____

_____

_____

_____

For Further Study:

- Using the method outlined in Study No. 8, "Beauty in the Works," do a topical study of the fool. What is he? How does he act? What are the results of his foolishness? How, specifically, does the foolish woman behave? List the ways in which you are acting like the fool, and resolve to engage in activities that will help you become a woman of wisdom and discretion.

The Pig and the Fool

Gold Ring in Pig's Nose	Reference	Beautiful Woman Without Discretion
Out of place, inappropriate	Ezekiel 28:17	
On animal heading for death	Proverbs 21:16	
Wasted; ring could be of value to someone else	Proverbs 12:15	
Of no value to pig	Proverbs 21:20	
Doesn't improve the appeal of the pig	1 Peter 3:3-4	
Doesn't disguise the pig's "pigness"	Proverbs 27:22 and 12:23	
Covered with mud and filth	Proverbs 26:11	
Pig cannot earn or purchase the ring	Psalm 100:3	
Only an outward ornament	Proverbs 31:30	
Anyone trying to gain the ring will have to join the pig in the mire	Proverbs 2:18-19 and 13:20	

The Pig and the Foolish Woman

Pig	Reference	Reference	Foolish Woman
	Leviticus 11:7 Deut. 14:8	Proverbs 5:8 1 Kings 11:1-11	
	Matthew 7:6	Proverbs 5:3-6	
	Psalm 80:8-13	Proverbs 14:1 Prov. 31:3	
Eats a lot		Proverbs 15:14	
Not selective in what it eats		Proverbs 9:14-18	
Knows nothing		Proverbs 9:13	
Never satisfied		Proverbs 17:24	
Noisy		Proverbs 18:2	
Content in mire		Proverbs 15:21	
Destructive in its rooting		Proverbs 12:4 Prov. 23:28	

Study No.3
Beauty and the Pit

"The mouth of strange women is a deep pit:
he that is abhorred of the LORD shall fall therein."
(Proverbs 22:14)

"Who can find a virtuous woman? for her price is far above rubies."
(Proverbs 31:10)

Scripture offers a detailed and colorful picture of two very different sorts of women. While offering wise and godly counsel to young men, the writers of the Book of Proverbs praise one kind of woman and warn against the other. The purpose of this study is to examine what God says about both women – the virtuous woman who fears and honors God, and the strange woman whose heart is bent on unfaithfulness and adultery.

A truly beautiful young lady will bring her attitudes and actions under the lordship of Jesus Christ. Her clothing, her countenance, her words, and her behavior will exhibit reverence for God, respect for her parents, and sisterly deference to the young men around her. She will be growing in the Lord, becoming the kind of woman whose "worth is far above rubies."

This study may not be as applicable to young girls as it will be to older ones. After discussing it with your parents, you might choose to save this particular study until you are older.

1. Read the following passages, using the charts on the following pages to compare the virtuous woman with the strange woman:

    Proverbs 2:16-19
    Proverbs 5:1-6
    Proverbs 6:23-29
    Proverbs 7
    Proverbs 12:4
    Proverbs 31:10-31
    1 Corinthians 6:9-10
    1 Timothy 2:9-10
    1 Peter 3:3-5

2. Write a summary comparison of the two types of women.

    _____

    _____

    _____

The Virtuous Woman and Strange Woman

	Virtuous Woman	Strange Woman
Appearance		
Clothing		
Speech		
Actions		
Thoughts		

The Virtuous Woman and Strange Woman

	Virtuous Woman	Strange Woman
Attitude		
Her effect on man		
Relationship to her home		
Her future reward		
To what she is compared		

3. ★ Listed below are descriptive phrases from the book of Proverbs about the strange woman. Meditate on each phrase and answer each question. Ask for your parents' opinions about each question, too. They may see you differently than you are able to see yourself.

a. 7:5 "flattereth with her words" and 7:21 "much fair speech," "flattering of her lips"

- Am I inappropriately forward with verbal praise or open admiration of others?
- Do I insincerely compliment or admire others with the purpose of manipulating them or getting their attention and favor?

b. 7:10 "with the attire of an harlot and subtil of heart"

- What is my purpose in the way I choose to dress?
- Do I dress attractively or do I dress to attract?
- Do I seek to serve my Christian brothers and other boys and men by dressing in a manner that does not tempt them to lust?

c. 7:11 "loud"

- Do I seek attention by making loud and silly remarks in the company of others?
- Do I engage in loud and giddy giggling with other girls when in the company of young men?
- Am I overly forward with young men, taking too much initiative in relating to them in a way that is too familiar?

d. 7:11 "stubborn"

- Do I resist the leadership of my parents, teachers, and authorities?
- Do I have a quiet and submissive spirit?
- Do I insist on having my own way?
- Do I choose to sin, going against what I know to be right?

e. 7:11 "her feet abide not in her house"

- What is my attitude toward home? Do I enjoy being there?
- Do I seek ways to avoid being at home?
- Am I bored, restless, or discontent when home?
- Am I using my time at home in profitable pursuits that serve others and help me mature?

f. 7:13 "an impudent face" and 6:25 "take thee with her eyelids"

- Does my countenance reflect a submissive spirit or a stubborn, self-serving spirit?
- Do I express my resistance to authority with my countenance?
- Do I use my eyes and mouth as a means of flirting with young men?
- Am I forward and pushy with young men?

g. 7:16 "decked [her] bed with coverings of tapestry, with carved works, with fine linen of Egypt" and 7:17 "perfumed [her] bed with myrrh, aloes, and cinnamon"

- Do I seek to appeal to the physical senses of young men in ways that *do not* bring glory to God?
- Do I seek to draw the attention of others to myself with an over-emphasis on makeup, perfumes, jewelry, and clothing?

h. 7:19 **"For the goodman is not at home, he is gone a long journey."**
- What do I do when my parents are not at home?
- What do I do when I am not under the direct oversight of my parents or other authority?

i. 7:22 **"He goeth after her straightway."**
- Am I testing my ability to succeed in attracting the attention of men to myself?
- Do I make a "game" of conquering young men, gaining their attentions for my own selfish satisfaction?

j. 2:17 **"Forsaketh the guide of her youth, and forgetteth the covenant of her God."**
- Am I stepping out from under the authority of Scripture and my parents?
- Am I obeying what I know to be true and right in all areas of my life, and especially in the area of my relationship to young men?
- Am I behaving like a daughter of The King?

4. ★ Review the passages about the virtuous woman. On a separate piece of paper list each phrase that describes her. Following the same pattern used in Question No. 3, list each reference and the description that is given. Then formulate your own questions to match each phrase as an aid in comparing yourself to the virtuous woman. If you have difficulty writing the questions, ask one of your parents to write them for you. Answer each question honestly.

5. Scripture paints a vivid picture of the strange woman. Proverbs 5:3-4 says,

    "For the lips of a strange woman drop as an **honeycomb**, and her mouth is **smoother than oil**: But her end is **bitter as wormwood**, sharp as a **two-edged sword**."

a. Review what you know about honeycombs and honey. How could a strange woman's lips "drop as an honeycomb?"

    _____

    _____

b. Go into a room and close the door. Put hand lotion on your hands. Now open the door and go out. How can a strange woman's mouth be like your slippery hands on the doorknob?

    _____

    _____

c. Get your mother's approval before you try this one! Make a section of your kitchen floor pretty and shiny by polishing it with a bit of cooking oil. Pour a tablespoon of oil on the floor and spread it over the surface until it is all absorbed.

Does the floor look nice? Now carefully try to walk across that section of the floor. What happens? How can a strange woman's mouth be like this slippery floor? What would happen to someone unaware of the oil if they walked across the floor? Be sure to follow your mother's instructions for cleaning up the floor!

_____

_____

_____

d. Look up the word "wormwood" in the dictionary. What is it? How is it used? Research further in a Bible dictionary, herb book, encyclopedia, or other helpful resource. How could the results of associating with a strange woman be as "bitter as wormwood?"

_____

_____

_____

_____

e. Do some research on swords. What is the purpose of a **two-edged** sword? How is it used? How can the end of associating with a strange woman be as "sharp as a two-edged sword?"

_____

_____

_____

6. ★ Prayerfully review this entire lesson. Then list specific actions, attitudes and thoughts that you need to change to become the virtuous, god-fearing woman described in Scripture. Ask your parents for their opinions, as well.

_____

_____

_____

_____

7. Outline a **step-by-step** plan for changing in the areas you have listed. List specific actions and specific time frames. Share this plan with your parents and ask them to pray for you and to hold you accountable for completing this plan.

_____

_____

_____

_____

_____

_____

_____

For further study:

- Study the life of Rahab, a strange woman who repented and feared the Lord. Use the study methods outlined in Study No. 7, "Beauty on the Move."

- Compare the strange woman, as she is described in Proverbs 7, with wisdom, which is personified as a woman in Proverbs 8. Design a chart to help you organize your observations.

- Using the methods outlined in Study No. 4, "Beauty and the Drip," study the following words as they are associated with the strange woman described in Proverbs.

  - Flattery/flattereth (Proverbs 2:16, 6:24 and 7:5)
  - Subtil of heart (Proverbs 7:10)
  - Loud (Proverbs 7:11)
  - Stubborn (Proverbs 7:11)
  - Impudent (Proverbs 7:13)
  - Fair speech (Proverbs 7:21)
  - Forced (Proverbs 7:21)
  - Beauty (Proverbs 6:25)
  - Take (Proverbs 6:25)
  - Moveable (Proverbs 5:6)

Study No. 4
Beauty and the Drip

"A foolish son is the calamity of his father:
and the contentions of a wife are a continual dropping."

(Proverbs 19:13)

In this study you will learn how to use a concordance while studying the Bible's description of the "contentious woman." We will be conducting a word study of the word **contentious** as it is used by the writers of the book of Proverbs. A woman, young lady, or girl can be outwardly beautiful while revealing an ugly spirit through her words and actions.

Our goal, as we complete each of the studies in this book, is to become truly beautiful in the eyes of God. This study will help us understand one of the common ways women choose to be ugly. Other studies will help us examine true womanly beauty as God describes it.

To help you see the question portions of this study, a box ❑ appears next to each section that asks for a written response. Each time you see the box, you will need to mark the text in some way or supply an answer to a question.

Materials needed for this study:

- **Strong's Exhaustive Concordance** (If you are serious about studying the Bible, you will use this indispensable tool for the rest of your life. It is worth the small investment. If you do not own **Strong's** and do not choose to purchase it at this time, see if your church library owns one or if you can borrow one from someone else.)
- Notebook

A. How to Read a Concordance Listing:

1. References:

Words are listed alphabetically in a concordance. Look up the word **contentious** in **Strong's Exhaustive Concordance**. Below this word you will see the following:

Pr	21:19	with a *c'* and angry woman.	4066
	26:21	so is a *c'* man to kindle strife	"
	27:15	rainy day and a *c'* woman are alike	"
Ro	2: 8	But unto them that are *c'*	*1537, 2052*
1 Co	11:16	But if any man seem to be *c'*,	5380

2. Verse Quotations:

The abbreviation and numbers at the beginning of each line indicate the reference of each verse in which the word **contentious** is used. If you are unfamiliar with standard abbreviations for the books of the Bible, refer to the list of abbreviations provided at the beginning of the concordance. You may want to copy this list and keep it as a marker in your concordance while you are studying.

The words in the center of each line quote the portion of the verse that contains the word **contentious**.

❑ Which two verses use the word in reference to a contentious **woman**?

_____

_____

Pr	21:19	with a *c'* and angry woman.	4066
	26:21	so is a *c'* man to kindle strife	"
	27:15	rainy day and a *c'* woman are alike	"
Ro	2: 8	But unto them that are *c'*	*1537, 2052
1 Co	11:16	But if any man seem to be *c'*,	5380

Note that all words listed in **Strong's Exhaustive Concordance** are based on **The King James Version** of the Bible. To look up words from a different translation of the Bible requires a concordance that is designed for that specific translation. For our purposes, using a King James Version Bible will be simplest.

3. **Dictionary Numbers:**

The numbers listed at the end of each line are numbers that correspond to **definition numbers** at the back of **Strong's Exhaustive Concordance.** All three verses listed from Proverbs have the same number following them. This means that the same original Hebrew word was used in all three of these verses.

❑ What number has the concordance assigned to this word? _____

Pr	21:19	with a *c'* and angry woman.	4066
	26:21	so is a *c'* man to kindle strife	"
	27:15	rainy day and a *c'* woman are alike	"
Ro	2: 8	But unto them that are *c'*	*1537, 2052
1 Co	11:16	But if any man seem to be *c'*,	5380

4. **Hebrew or Greek?**

Numbers for references from the Old Testament are listed in standard type and indicate that these words will be listed in the **Hebrew** portion of the dictionary. This dictionary appears **first** at the back of **Strong's.**

Pr	21:19	with a *c'* and angry woman.	4066
	26:21	so is a *c'* man to kindle strife	"
	27:15	rainy day and a *c'* woman are alike	"
Ro	2: 8	But unto them that are *c'*	*1537, 2052
1 Co	11:16	But if any man seem to be *c'*,	5380

Numbers for New Testament references appear in italic type. These definitions will appear in the **Greek** dictionary, which follows the Hebrew one.

All **Old Testament words** will be defined in the **Hebrew dictionary**; all **New Testament words** will be defined in the **Greek dictionary**. The difference in type style for their numbers will help you remember this.

❑ Which dictionary will you use to look up the definition for Number 4066, as it is used in the verses from Proverbs?_____

Pr	21:19	with a *c'* and angry woman.	4066
	26:21	so is a *c'* man to kindle strife	"
	27:15	rainy day and a *c'* woman are alike	"
Ro	2: 8	But unto them that are *c'*	*1537, 2052*
1 Co	11:16	But if any man seem to be *c'*,	*5380*

Searching for a definition of an Old Testament word in the Greek dictionary can lead to confusion! For instance, if you looked up **4066** (the number for **contentious** as used in the Old Testament verses) in the **Greek** dictionary instead of the Hebrew, you would find a definition relating to "region" or "country." You might wonder what that has to do with a contentious lady!

B. How to Read a Dictionary Entry

Look up Number 4066 in the **Hebrew dictionary**. You will find the following listing:

> **4066.** מָדוֹן **madown,** *maw-dohn'*; from 1777; a *contest* or quarrel:
> -- brawling, contention (-ous), discord, strife. Comp. 4079, 4090

1. Original Hebrew Word

Following the number is the original word as it is written in Hebrew.

❑ Circle or highlight this word.

> **4066.** מָדוֹן **madown,** *maw-dohn'*; from 1777; a *contest* or quarrel:
> -- brawling, contention (-ous), discord, strife. Comp. 4079, 4090

2. English Equivalent:

Immediately following is the exact equivalent of the word in English letters.

❑ Circle or highlight this word.

> **4066.** מָדוֹן **madown,** *maw-dohn'*; from 1777; a *contest* or quarrel:
> -- brawling, contention (-ous), discord, strife. Comp. 4079, 4090

3. English Pronunciation:

Next follows the precise pronunciation of the Hebrew word, using standard English pronunciation markings.

❑ Circle or highlight this pronunciation.

> **4066.** מָדוֹן **madown,** *maw-dohn'*; from 1777; a *contest* or quarrel:
> -- brawling, contention (-ous), discord, strife. Comp. 4079, 4090

4. Word History

After the pronunciation, the "etymology" of the word is given. This is the history of the word, tracing it back to its root word or words. In this case, **madown** comes from the root word 1777 **diyn** or **duwn**. This information is useful because the study of the root words can often give a fuller understanding of the word being studied.

❑ Circle or highlight this listing.

> **4066.** מָדוֹן **madown,** *maw-dohn'*; from 1777; a *contest* or quarrel:
> -- brawling, contention (-ous), discord, strife. Comp. 4079, 4090

5. Meaning of the Word

Next the concise meaning of the word is listed. This portion ends with a colon (:)

❑ Circle or highlight this portion.

> **4066.** מָדוֹן **madown,** *maw-dohn'*; from 1777; a *contest* or quarrel:
> -- brawling, contention (-ous), discord, strife. Comp. 4079, 4090

6. English Renderings of the Hebrew Word

Following the meaning, the colon, and the dash mark (: --), are all the different English renderings of the original Hebrew word. These are the different words that the translators of the **King James Version** chose to use when translating this particular Hebrew word into English. For this Hebrew word, the translators chose the words **brawling, contention, contentious, discord,** and **strife.** The syllable "-ous" that is enclosed in parentheses after the word **contention** indicates that the adjective, or descriptive, form of the word [contentious] is also rendered from the Hebrew **madown.**

❑ Circle or highlight this portion.

> **4066.** מָדוֹן **madown,** *maw-dohn'*; from 1777; a *contest* or quarrel:
> -- brawling, contention (-ous), discord, strife. Comp. 4079, 4090

7. Additional Notes

The last listing in this particular dictionary entry is comparing this Hebrew word with Numbers 4079 and 4090. Both of these words are other Hebrew forms of the same word. It is often useful to also study these words to gain a better understanding of the main word being studied.

❑ Circle or highlight this portion on the following page.

4066. מָדוֹן madown, *maw-dohn'*; from 1777; a *contest* or quarrel:
-- brawling, contention (-ous), discord, strife. Comp. 4079, 4090

Many abbreviations appear in the dictionary entries. An explanation of these abbreviations is listed at the beginning of the dictionary, before the alphabetical listing of words and definitions. This will help you if you do not understand a particular dictionary entry.

C. How To Do Your Word Study

1. **Studying the word "contentious"**

   a. For our study we will only be studying the Hebrew word that is used in the verses from Proverbs. **Because all three verses are followed by the same number (4066), we know that the same original Hebrew word was used in all three verses.**

   ❑ Using your notebook, label four separate pages as follows:

   1. How Does a Contentious Person Behave?

   2. To What Is a Contentious Person Likened?

   3. How Should a Contentious Person Be Treated?

   4. What Happens to a Contentious Person?

   b. ❑ First, review the definition **madown**, the Hebrew word for contentious. What does the word mean?

   _____

   ❑ Does this tell you something about the way a contentious person behaves? Note this on the page you labeled "How Does a Contentious Person Behave?"

   c. Now read each of the three verses from Proverbs, and note your observations on the labeled pages. For instance, Proverbs 21:19 reads, *"It is better to dwell in the wilderness, than with a contentious and an angry woman."* This particular verse is a little difficult to categorize according to our four page headings. We have to think a bit.

   Does the verse tell us how the contentious woman acts? Perhaps. We get the idea that she isn't very pleasant to be around, but the verse does not actually tell us about her actions.

   Does the verse liken the contentious woman to any other person or object? No.

   Does the verse tell us how we should treat a contentious person? No. It does describe what is naturally preferable to living with a contentious and angry woman, but it doesn't tell us that we **should** go live in the wilderness to avoid her.

   Does the verse describe what happens to a contentious person? No.

Given the four categories that we have selected, this verse seems to fit best under the heading, "How Does a Contentious Person Behave?" We could say, "She acts in a manner that makes people not want to be with her."

❑ Write this or your own words on page one of your notes.

d. Proverbs 26:21 states, "As coals are to burning coals, and wood to fire; so is a contentious man to kindle strife."

What does this verse tell us about a contentious person? It compares him to "coals...to burning coals" and "wood to fire." What happens to one piece of barbecue briquet when it comes in contact with others that are already burning? What happens to a piece of wood when it is added to a fire? The Bible tells us that the contentious person is like these objects. Just like the fresh coal and wood kindle the fire, so a contentious person is sure to kindle strife. He stirs up discord.

❑ What can you write on your page, "To What Is a Contentious Person Likened?"

❑ What can you write on the page, "How Does the Contentious Person Behave?"

e. ❑ Proverbs 27:15 should be easy. Read the verse and record your observations on the appropriate page in your notebook.

2. Finding Other English Translations of the Hebrew Word:

We have now read all the verses that contained the Hebrew word that was translated as "contentious." To continue our study, we will return to the definition of the word, Number 4066, as it was given in the Hebrew word dictionary.

> **4066.** מָדוֹן **madown,** *maw-dohn'*; from 1777; a *contest* or quarrel:
> -- brawling, contention (-ous), discord, strife. Comp. 4079, 4090

In order to study more passages in the Bible that contain this same Hebrew word, **madown,** we will look at the other English renderings of the word as they are translated in the **King James Version**. These words are all listed after the dash (--).

❑ List these words:

_____   _____

_____   _____

3. How to Look Up Verses That All Use the Same Hebrew Word:

a. Go back to the concordance and look up the word **brawling**. It will look like this:

| Pr | 21: 9 | with a *b* woman in a wide house. | *4090 |
| Pr | 25:24 | with a *b* woman in a wide house. | *4090 |

❑ What are the references for the verses that are followed by the number 4066?

_____

As you can see, there are **no** verses that use the word numbered 4066.

❑ What number is shown for the word **brawling**?

_____

Look back at the **dictionary** entry for No. 4066. Notice the last three words in that definition. They read:

"Comp. 4079, 4090."

Do you remember what these words mean? Both of these numbers represent other Hebrew forms of the word **madown**, No. 4066.

Locate No. 4090 in the Hebrew dictionary in the back of **Strong's Exhaustive Concordance**. The entry looks like this:

4090. מָדוֹן **medan**, _med-awn'_; a form of 4066: -- discord, strife

This word is simply another Hebrew form of No. 4066. Both words have the same meaning.

❑ Read both of the verses listed under the word **brawling**. Using your notebook, record your observations on the appropriate pages. Do these verses answer any of our four questions? 1. How Does a Contentious Person Behave? 2. To What Is a Contentious Person Likened? 3. How Should a Contentious Person Be Treated? 4. What Happens to a Contentious Person?

_b._ Go back to the concordance and look up the word **contention**. It will look like this:

Pr	13:10	by pride cometh _c_ : but with the	4683
	17:14	leave off _c_ , before it be meddled	7379
	18: 6	A fool's lips enter into _c_ , and his	"
	22:10	out the scorner, and _c_ shall go out:	4066
Jer	15:10	a man of _c_ to the whole earth!	"
Hab	1: 3	there are that raise up strife and _c_ .	"
Ac	15:39	And the _c_ was so sharp between	3948
Ph'p	1:16	The one preach Christ of _c_ , not	*2051
1 Th	2: 2	the gospel of God with much _c_ .	* 78

❑ What 3 verses are followed by the number 4066?

_____

_____

_____

❏ Read each of these three verses and record any observations on the appropriate four pages of your notebook. 1. How Does a Contentious Person Behave? 2. To What Is a Contentious Person Likened? 3. How Should a Contentious Person Be Treated? 4. What Happens to a Contentious Person?

c. The next word listed in the dictionary as an English translation of No. 4066, **madown**, is **discord**. Locate this word in your concordance. The entry will look like this..

| Pr | 6:14 | continually ; he soweth *d* . | 4066 |
| | :19 | that soweth *d* among brethren | 4090 |

❏ Read both of these verses and record any observations on the appropriate four pages of your notebook.

d. The last English translation listed for the Hebrew word **madown** is **strife**. There is a long listing of verses for this word. Look for all the verses that are followed by the number 4066. Listed below are the lines from this entry that are pertinent to our study.

Ps	80: 6	us a s unto our neighbours	4066
Pr	15:18	A wrathful man stirreth up *s* :	4066
	16:28	A forward man soweth *s* : and a	4066
	17:14	The beginning of *s* is as when one	4066
	26:20	is no talebearer, the *s* ceaseth.	*4066
	28:25	is of a proud heart stirreth up *s* :	4066

❏ Read each of these verses and record any observations on the appropriate four pages of your notebook.

❏ After reviewing the notes that you have recorded in your notebook, write a summary paragraph answering each of these four questions:

How does the contentious person behave?

_____

_____

_____

_____

_____

To what is the contentious person likened?

_____

_____

_____

_____

_____

How should the contentious person be treated?

_____

_____

_____

_____

_____

_____

_____

What happens to a contentious person?

_____

_____

_____

_____

_____

_____

D. Obeying God's Word

1. Examining Our Lives

Pray, asking God to help you see yourself as He does.

❑ In what ways do you behave like a contentious person? Be specific. Think about your relationship with God, parents, siblings, other family members, friends, and teachers.

_____

_____

_____

_____

_____

2. Repenting

Confess these sins to God and ask His forgiveness.

❑ Do you need to confess your sin to others and ask their forgiveness? List the names of those you need to contact.

_____

_____

_____

_____

3. Demonstrating Fruits of Repentance

Ephesians 4:22-24 says,

"That ye put off concerning the former conversation the old man, which is corrupt according to the deceitful lusts; and be renewed in the spirit of your mind; and that ye put on the new man, which after God is created in righteousness and true holiness."

❑ You may be recognizing that you need to put off the "old man" of contention. Now, what will you put **on**? List at least 4 specific actions that you will take to obey God in this area. Share your commitment with your parents, and ask them to pray for you and hold you accountable.

_____

_____

_____

_____

_____

_____

For Further Study:

• What is the opposite of contention? Use your concordance and the method outlined in this chapter to study this trait.

• The Bible says that the contentious person is a proud person. Do a topical study on **pride,** following the basic method outlined in Study No. 8, "Beauty in the Works."

Study No. 5

Beauty in the Heart

"Whose adorning
let it not be that outward adorning
of plaiting the hair, and of wearing of gold,
or of putting on of apparel;

But let it be the hidden man of the heart,
in that which is not corruptible,
even the ornament of a meek and quiet spirit,
which is in the sight of God of great price."

(1 Peter 3:3–4)

The Bible offers beauty advice to young ladies and women. It tells us what will truly be an ornament of beauty for any woman, whether she was born with a pretty face or not. This ornament creates the kind of beauty that is precious in God's eyes.

God wants us to reflect His glory and beauty even in how we dress and how we care for our bodies. Braided hair, jewelry, and beautiful garments *can* reflect our submissive spirit before God, our parents, and our husbands. God does, however, warn us to not put our *focus* on these areas. True beauty is not just on the outside. Jesus accused the Pharisees of being "like unto whited sepulchres, which indeed appear beautiful outward, but are within full of dead men's bones, and of all uncleanness" (Matthew 23:27).

A beautiful woman can be a "whitewashed tomb," attractive on the outside, but disgusting on the inside. True beauty is an attitude of the heart, which is reflected in our actions. A beautiful, God-fearing heart will show on the outside, too!

In this study we will learn how to study a single verse or short passage of Scripture. We will also learn how to use the marginal references that are in most Bibles.

A. Studying the Text

1. Copy 1 Peter 3:3-4.

_____

_____

_____

_____

_____

_____

_____

_____

2. With a blue pencil, mark all the words in this passage that tell a woman how to adorn herself. With a red pencil, mark the words that tell a woman how **not** to adorn herself.

3. Read these verses from several other translations.

4. Read the verses within their context by reading 1 Peter 2:13-3:9.

5. Summarize 1 Peter 2:13-17. What is its message?

_____

_____

_____

_____

_____

6. Assign this passage a title. What short phrase would best describe its message?

_____

7. Summarize 1 Peter 2:18-25. What is its message?

_____

_____

_____

_____

_____

8. Assign this passage a title. What short phrase would best describe its message?

_____

9. What is the first word (or phrase, if you are not using the King James Version) of 1 Peter 3:1?

_____

10. What does this word (or phrase) mean? _____

11. To what is this word (or phrase) referring?

_____

_____

_____

12. Summarize 1 Peter 3:1-7. What is its message?

_____

_____

_____

_____

_____

13. Assign this passage a title. What short phrase would best describe its message?

_____

14. Summarize 1 Peter 3:8-9. If you are reading from the King James Version, you will notice that these verses begin with the word "finally." The New American Standard Version uses the phrase, "to sum up." This indicates that the next words are going to help us summarize all that has been said up to this point. What is the message of these two verses?

_____

_____

_____

15. Assign this passage a title. What short phrase would best describe its message?

_____

16. How does 1 Peter 3:1-9 relate to 1 Peter 2:13-25?

_____

_____

_____

17. Take notes on 1 Peter 3:1-9, and outline the passage, listing main points, with the sub-points below each point.

_____

_____

_____

_____

_____

_____

_____

_____

_____

_____

_____

_____

_____

_____

_____

_____

B. How to Use Marginal References

1. To examine the text of verses 3 and 4 more carefully, we will look at your Bible's marginal references. Many styles of marginal references, or cross references, exist. These notes are very helpful and easy to use. The easiest way to understand a Bible's system of cross referencing is to look through the beginning pages of the Bible for the section that explains its particular cross referencing system.

Look carefully at 1 Peter 3:3-4 in your Bible. Besides the obvious text of the verses and the verse numbers, do you see any other small numbers or letters in the verses? Many Bibles also have a column of small words along one margin or between the two columns of Scripture text.

2. If your Bible does not include any of these features, examine other Bibles in your home until you find one with marginal references. If you can see examples in an actual Bible, the explanation offered here will be easier to understand.

3. Most Bibles with marginal references mark words and phrases within the verse with "superior" numbers and letters. "Superior" simply means that the letters and numbers are smaller and raised higher than the rest of the type in the text.

   In the page's reference column, on one side or the other of the text, or in between the two columns of text, bold numbers will indicate verse numbers, and after each verse number will appear any notes pertaining to that particular verse.

   For instance, in the **International Inductive Study Bible,** 1 Peter 3:3 has a superior "a" at the beginning of it. The marginal notes list, after the bold number **3,**

   "a. Is. 3:18ff; 1 Tim. 2:9."

   These verses relate to the words in verse 3 of 1 Peter 3. The "ff" following "Is. 3:18" means that we should read Isaiah 3:18 and the verses following.

   Read Isaiah 3:18 and following, and 1 Timothy 2:9. What do these verses say? How do they relate to 1 Peter 3:3?

   _____

   _____

   _____

   _____

4. Verse 4 in the same Bible has a superior "a" before the words "the hidden person." The marginal notes, after the bold number **4,** read:

   "Rom. 7:22"

   Read Romans 7:22. What does this verse tell us about the "hidden person?"

   _____

   _____

5. In another Bible the phrase "plaiting the hair" in 1 Peter 3:3 is explained as "arranging," and the word "apparel" is clarified as "fine apparel" in the cross references. These notes help us better understand the meaning of the passage.

In verse 4, a cross reference defines "meek" as "gentle," and "of great price" as "precious."

One word of caution is needed. It is important to remember that marginal notes are **not the divinely inspired Word of God**. They are editors' notes, written by scholars who have studied the Bible and its original languages. These notes are not infallible. They are influenced by the editors' theology. They are influenced by different understandings of the same word.

For instance, the word "gentle" is used to clarify the meaning of "meek." What does gentle mean? Jesus was "meek." Was he always "gentle?" It depends on one's definition of gentleness. The moneychangers in the temple probably didn't think he was very gentle. Meekness encompasses much more than a mild-mannered gentleness.

Marginal notes can help us understand the meanings of words, but the best way to understand a word's meaning is to study how the same word is used in other passages of the Bible. You have learned how to study words in Study No. 4, "Beauty and the Drip." Taking the time to study words in this way will deepen your understanding of and love for Scripture.

6. Some Bibles do not use marginal references and simply list each note at the end of the verse text. If a small superior **1** is in the verse text; a note, in smaller type, will appear after the verse, preceded by the number **1**.

Other Bibles simply list additional references, in small type, after the text of each individual verse. No superior numbers or letters appear in the text, and the notes are not numbered. Any notes following verse 3 pertain to verse 3, and any notes following verse 4 pertain to verse 4.

Other Bibles simply mark a word within the verse's text with a small "R" or "T." The "R" indicates that another Bible reference, in smaller type, will follow the verse text. If you look up this verse, you will find that its content relates to the verse you are studying. The "T" indicates that notes about the following word will be at the end of the verse.

For instance, the **Open Bible**, published by Thomas Nelson, in 1 Peter 3:4, places an "R" in front of the words "the hidden person." At the end of the verse, in small letters, is the reference "Romans 2:29." This verse also teaches us about the inner man, and will help you better understand what Peter is telling us about in 1 Peter 3:4.

Read Romans 2:29. What does it say and how does it relate to I Peter 3:4?

_____

_____

_____

7. This same Bible also places a small "T" before the word "incorruptible." Looking at the end of the verse, we see, in italics, the word "imperishable." This word helps us better understand the meaning of "incorruptible."

8. If we go on to 1 Peter 3:6 in **The Open Bible**, an "R" appears before the phrase "calling him lord." At the end of the verse, we see a note that says, "Gen. 18:12."

   Read Genesis 18:12. What does this verse say? How does it relate to 1 Peter 3:6?

   _____

   _____

   _____

   This demonstrates another helpful feature of marginal references. The Bible often quotes itself. It is filled with references to Old Testament stories and events. Marginal notes help us easily locate these quotes and stories.

9. As you can see, all formats of marginal referencing are working with the same basic principles. Notes are arranged in a manner that enables you to read other Scripture passages related to the same topic. This will help you in your study.

   Look at your Bible, and notice any marginal notes it contains on 1 Peter 3:1-8. Do they contain any other information that we have not already seen in the examples given in this section? If so, read the verses and explanations and note anything new you have learned.

   _____

   _____

   _____

C. Summarizing What We Have Learned

1. If there are any words in this passage that you still do not understand, look them up in your concordance, and read their definitions.

   List the words and their definitions below:

   _____

   _____

   _____

2. Review all that you have learned in this study. What is true beauty in God's eyes? What does it look like? What does it act like? What attitudes does it include?

_____

_____

_____

_____

_____

_____

_____

D. Applying What We Have Learned

1. ✯ What is the Holy Spirit saying to you through your study of 1 Peter 2:13-3:9? Does your life reflect a beauty that God values? In what areas do you need to change? Think about your relationship to the authorities in your life. Think about your attitudes and words toward your siblings and friends. Think about your attitude toward your outward appearance. Be specific.

_____

_____

_____

_____

_____

2. List at least 4 specific actions you will commit to do in obedience to God's Word over the next week. List specific people, specific actions, and specific times. Don't just focus on what you will quit doing. What will you **do**? Ask your parents to pray for you and hold you accountable.

_____

_____

_____

For Further Study:

- Study the meanings of the words **meek**, **meekness** and **quiet** (as used in 1 Peter 3:4). Then study the word **subjection** as it is used in 1 Peter 3:1 and 5. How is a meek and quiet spirit related to godly subjection? Use your concordance and the method outlined in Study No. 4, "Beauty and the Drip."

- Study the lives of those that are identified in Scripture as **meek**. Use the character study method as outlined in Study No. 7, "Beauty on the Move."

- In Matthew 11:29, Jesus tells us, "Take my yoke upon you, and learn of me; for I am meek and lowly in heart: and ye shall find rest unto your souls." Study the life of Jesus. How was his meekness demonstrated?

- Study Matthew 11:29 in the same way we studied 1 Peter 3:1-6. What does Jesus mean? What is "rest unto your souls?"

- What promises are given to the meek? Use your concordance and topical Bible to answer this question. Make a list of all the promises.

- Study Genesis 24:53, Psalm 45:8-14, Proverbs 31:22, and Ezekiel 16:10-17. What can we learn from these passages? Does God disapprove of outward adornment?

Study No. 6
Beauty and the Feast

*"For Esther did the commandment of Mordecai,
like as when she was brought up with him."*

(Esther 2:20b)

Esther was a beautiful woman – the most beautiful in all the Persian Empire, according to the judgment of King Ahasuerus. Esther 2:7 says, "...And the maid was fair and beautiful." The Hebrew word that is translated "fair" in this verse (yapheh) is the same word that is used in Proverbs to describe our "fair woman which is without discretion."

In the book of Esther we are privileged to observe a fair woman whose attitudes and actions exhibit good judgment and discretion. Esther was also a woman of courage. She understood authority, she understood human nature, and she used wise judgment while risking her life to save the lives of her people.

While studying the life and example of Esther, we will learn how to study an entire book of the Bible. We will focus on the first eight chapters. You will need some colored pencils or pens.

A good student of the Bible, as he reads, will look for the answers to six important questions. These questions are often referred to as the "who-what-when" questions, or the "5 W's and an H" questions.

WHO? Who is in the story?

WHAT? What happened in the story? What were people trying to do in the story?

WHEN? When did the story take place? When did different events take place in the story?

WHERE? Where did the story take place? Where did different events in the story occur?

WHY? Why did a person do what he did? Why did he say what he said? Why did he think what he thought? Why did certain events occur?

HOW? How did an event happen? How did people know the things they knew? How long did events take to happen?

We will learn how to answer these questions as we study the book of Esther.

1. **Read each chapter of Esther.** This exercise may take several study sessions. The entire text of Esther, in the King James Version, is included on pages 55 through 66. Your observations will help you better understand the story, will help you notice details you might have otherwise overlooked, and will help you easily identify the actions and words of the story's various characters. If you are a young Bible student, or if this exercise becomes

too tedious after you have begun, just read the story carefully, trying to give special attention to the categories listed below.

A. Mark the mention of each **main person** in the story in a particular way. Use a different color of pencil to highlight each person's name, or draw some simple picture that identifies each person.

B. With the same colors, **underline** the **actions** and **words** of each person. What did each person do? What did he or she say?

C. Mark every mention of **time** in a special way. Circle the words with a special color or label them with a simple drawing of a clock.

D. Mark each mention of **location** – where an action or event takes place, where a person was, etc. (Draw a box around the words or label with a simple drawing of a road sign.)

E. Answer the following "why" and "how" questions:

Why did the king call Vashti to appear at his feast? _____

_____

Why was King Ahasuerus angry with Queen Vashti? _____

_____

Why were the men of the kingdom concerned about Vashti's actions? _____

_____

Why did Esther conceal the fact that she was a Jew? _____

_____

Why were Bigthan and Teresh hanged?_____

_____

Why was Haman angry with Mordecai?_____

_____

How did Haman seek to punish Mordecai?_____

Why did Mordecai wear sackcloth and ashes? _____

_____

Why was Esther reluctant to go before the king to plead for her people?_____

_____

Why did Haman have a gallows made? _____

Why did the king want to honor Mordecai? _____

_____

Why did Haman's wife say that Haman would fall before Mordecai? _____

_____

Why was Haman afraid when Esther accused him before the king at the second banquet?

_____

How was Haman killed? _____

How were the Jews saved from destruction? _____

_____

2. Read the entire book of Esther (pages 55- 66). Assign a title to each chapter – a short group of words that summarizes the main events or thoughts of the chapter. Write your title above each chapter and in the chart below. Also select one or two words that describe Esther's character as it is displayed in the events of each chapter. Was she brave? Prudent? Obedient? Write your descriptive words next to your chapter titles below.

Chapter	Title	Description of Esther
One	_____	_____
Two	_____	_____
Three	_____	_____
Four	_____	_____
Five	_____	_____
Six	_____	_____
Seven	_____	_____
Eight	_____	_____
Nine	_____	_____
Ten	_____	(not present in this chapter)

3. Write a short summary of the story of Esther. What happens in the story?

_____

_____

_____

_____

_____

4. Review each chapter, looking for all references to Esther. Using the chart on the following page, note how Esther related to each main character in the story, and how each of these people responded to her.

5. Read Esther 2:20. Why do you think Esther obeyed Mordecai, even after she became queen?

_____

_____

6. Mordecai, Esther's cousin, was acting as her adopted father. Do you think Esther's habit of obedience affected her actions as a young woman suddenly placed into the king's court? Why do you think she found favor in the eyes of Hegai, in the eyes of the maidens and eunuchs, and in the eyes of the king?

_____

_____

_____

_____

7. Read Esther 1:9-12. How does Vashti's response to the king compare with Esther's responses to the different authorities in her life? How do their actions and attitudes differ?

_____

_____

_____

_____

Esther's Relationships to Other People in the Story

	Esther toward person(s)	Person(s) toward Esther
Mordecai		
Hegai		
Maidens and eunuchs		
King Ahasuerus		
Haman		

8. Read the fourth chapter of Esther. When Mordecai asked her to go before the king, what did Esther do? What did she ask Mordecai to do?

_____

_____

_____

9. Read about Esther's first banquet in Esther 5:6-8. Study Esther's words to the king; then list the words and phrases that reflect her respect for him.

_____

_____

_____

10. Review chapters 1-3 of Esther and note the actions and attitudes of King Ahasuerus. List each observation below.

   a. _____

   b. _____

   c. _____

   d. _____

   e. _____

   f. _____

   g. _____

   h. _____

11. Review chapters 1-3 once more and note the actions and attitudes of Haman. List your observations below:

   a. _____

   b. _____

   c. _____

   d. _____

   e. _____

f. _____

g. _____

h. _____

12. Study and analyze Esther's actions. Why did she invite Haman to the banquet? In light of what you have observed in Questions 10 and 11, why do you think she chose to ask Haman and the king to a second banquet? What could she have recognized in the characters of both King Ahasuerus and Haman that might have led her to invite them to a second banquet before she appealed to the king?

_____

_____

_____

13. Read Esther 5:9-6:14. List the events that occur between Esther's first and second banquets. Pay special attention to Haman's words, attitudes, and actions.

a. _____

b. _____

c. _____

d. _____

e. _____

f. _____

g. _____

h. _____

i. _____

j. _____

k. _____

l. _____

m. _____

n. _____

o. _____

p. _____

q. _____

r. _____

s. _____

t. _____

14. Summarize Haman's character as it is revealed in the observations listed above.

_____

_____

_____

_____

15. Study Esther's words at the second banquet (Esther 7:1-6). How does she appeal to the king?

_____

_____

_____

16. How does the king respond?

_____

_____

_____

17. How does Haman respond? What happens to him?

_____

_____

_____

18. Read the following Proverbs. How does each relate to the story of Haman's life?

Proverbs 11:2

_____

Proverbs 15:25

_____

_____

Proverbs 16:18

_____

_____

19. Because our purpose in studying the book of Esther is to learn more about true beauty and godly discretion as seen in Esther's life, we will not study the rest of the book in great detail. Summarize below what happens after Haman is hanged.

_____

_____

_____

_____

_____

_____

20. Even though God is not specifically mentioned in the book of Esther, His presence and sovereign control are obvious. In what ways did God sovereignly intervene to preserve His people?

_____

_____

_____

21. What can we learn from the life of Esther? How did she respond to authority? Notice the repeated use of the word "if" in her appeals. How did she react to a life-threatening situation? How did she decide what to do? What wisdom did she show in her plans?

_____

_____

_____

22. ⭐ In Esther's life, we can see the beauty of obedience, trusting the authorities over us, discretion, respectful appeal, patience, courage, understanding of the character of others, and the wise use of the opportunities, position, and talents that God grants us. In what areas can you be more like Esther? What qualities can you emulate?

_____

_____

_____

23. What definite plan of action will you commit to do to bring change in your life?

_____

_____

_____

_____

_____

For further study:

- Read Esther aloud with your family. Assign people to read specific parts: narrator, Esther, Mordecai, Haman, Ahasuerus, the king's wise men and attendants.

- Read Esther again, with your father reading aloud. Following the tradition of the Jewish Purim, arm the rest of the family with various noisemakers – pots and pans and spoons, whistles, etc. Every time Haman's name is read, blot it out with your noisemakers.

- Contrast the lives of Haman and Mordecai. What can you learn from the example of both of these men?

- Note all the feasts in the book of Esther. Mark each mention of a feast throughout the text, and then list them. Is there any special significance apparent in the many feasts listed?

- Note the use of the word "favor" in the book of Esther. Mark the word each time it is mentioned in the text. Using the word study method outlined in Study No. 4, "Beauty and the Drip," find out what original Hebrew word(s) were used in these passages. Is it the same word that is used in Proverbs 31: 30, which states that "favor is deceitful?" Study other uses of the word "favor" throughout Scripture.

The Book of Esther

Chapter 1 _____

1 Now it came to pass in the days of Ahasuerus, (this is Ahasuerus which reigned, from India even unto Ethiopia, over an hundred and seven and twenty provinces:)

2 That in those days, when the king Ahasuerus sat on the throne of his kingdom, which was in Shushan the palace,

3 In the third year of his reign, he made a feast unto all his princes and his servants; the power of Persia and Media, the nobles and princes of the provinces, being before him:

4 When he showed the riches of his glorious kingdom and the honour of his excellent majesty many days, even an hundred and fourscore days.

5 And when these days were expired, the king made a feast unto all the people that were present in Shushan the palace, both unto great and small, seven days, in the court of the garden of the king's palace;

6 Where were white, green, and blue, hangings, fastened with cords of fine linen and purple to silver rings and pillars of marble: the beds were of gold and silver, upon a pavement of red, and blue, and white, and black, marble.

7 And they gave them drink in vessels of gold, (the vessels being diverse one from another,) and royal wine in abundance, according to the state of the king.

8 And the drinking was according to the law; none did compel: for so the king had appointed to all the officers of his house, that they should do according to every man's pleasure.

9 Also Vashti the queen made a feast for the women in the royal house which belonged to king Ahasuerus.

10 On the seventh day, when the heart of the king was merry with wine, he commanded Mehuman, Biztha, Harbona, Bigtha, and Abagtha, Zethar, and Carcas, the seven chamberlains that served in the presence of Ahasuerus the king,

11 To bring Vashti the queen before the king with the crown royal, to show the people and the princes her beauty: for she was fair to look on.

12 But the queen Vashti refused to come at the king's commandment by his chamberlains: therefore was the king very wroth, and his anger burned in him.

13 Then the king said to the wise men, which knew the times, (for so was the king's manner toward all that knew law and judgment:

14 And the next unto him was Carshena, Shethar, Admatha, Tarshish, Meres, Marsena, and Memucan, the seven princes of Persia and Media, which saw the king's face, and which sat the first in the kingdom;)

15 What shall we do unto the queen Vashti according to law, because she hath not performed the commandment of the king Ahasuerus by the chamberlains?

16 And Memucan answered before the king and the princes, Vashti the queen hath not done wrong to the king only, but also to all the princes, and to all the people that are in all the provinces of the king Ahasuerus.

17 For this deed of the queen shall come abroad unto all women, so that they shall despise their husbands in their eyes, when it shall be reported, The king Ahasuerus commanded Vashti the queen to be brought in before him, but she came not.

18 Likewise shall the ladies of Persia and Media say this day unto all the king's princes, which have heard of the deed of the queen. Thus shall there arise too much contempt and wrath.

19 If it please the king, let there go a royal commandment from him, and let it be written among the laws of the Persians and the Medes, that it be not altered, That Vashti come no more before king Ahasuerus; and let the king give her royal estate unto another that is better than she.

20 And when the king's decree which he shall make shall be published throughout all his empire, (for it is great,) all the wives shall give to their husbands honour, both to great and small.

21 And the saying pleased the king and the princes; and the king did according to the word of Memucan:

22 For he sent letters into all the king's provinces, into every province according to the writing thereof, and to every people after their language, that every man should bear rule in his own house, and that it should be published according to the language of every people.

Chapter 2 _____

1 After these things, when the wrath of king Ahasuerus was appeased, he remembered Vashti, and what she had done, and what was decreed against her.

2 Then said the king's servants that ministered unto him, Let there be fair young virgins sought for the king:

3 And let the king appoint officers in all the provinces of his kingdom, that they may gather together all the fair young virgins unto Shushan the palace, to the house of the women, unto the custody of Hege the king's chamberlain, keeper of the women; and let their things for purification be given them:

4 And let the maiden which pleaseth the king be queen instead of Vashti. And the thing pleased the king; and he did so.

5 Now in Shushan the palace there was a certain Jew, whose name was Mordecai, the son of Jair, the son of Shimei, the son of Kish, a Benjamite;

6 Who had been carried away from Jerusalem with the captivity which had been carried away with Jeconiah king of Judah, whom Nebuchadnezzar the king of Babylon had carried away.

7 And he brought up Hadassah, that is, Esther, his uncle's daughter: for she had neither father nor mother, and the maid was fair and beautiful; whom Mordecai, when her father and mother were dead, took for his own daughter.

8 So it came to pass, when the king's commandment and his decree was heard, and when many maidens were gathered together unto Shushan the palace, to the custody of Hegai, that Esther was brought also unto the king's house, to the custody of Hegai, keeper of the women.

9 And the maiden pleased him, and she obtained kindness of him; and he speedily gave her her things for purification, with such things as belonged to her, and seven maidens, which were meet to be given her, out of the king's house: and he preferred her and her maids unto the best place of the house of the women.

10 Esther had not showed her people nor her kindred: for Mordecai had charged her that she should not show it.

11 And Mordecai walked every day before the court of the women's house, to know how Esther did, and what should become of her.

12 Now when every maid's turn was come to go in to king Ahasuerus, after that she had been twelve months, according to the manner of the women, (for so were the days of their purifications accomplished, to wit, six months with oil of myrrh, and six months with sweet odours, and with other things for the purifying of the women;)

13 Then thus came every maiden unto the king; whatsoever she desired was given her to go with her out of the house of the women unto the king's house.

14 In the evening she went, and on the morrow she returned into the second house of the women, to the custody of Shaashgaz, the king's chamberlain, which kept the concubines: she came in unto the king no more, except the king delighted in her, and that she were called by name.

15 Now when the turn of Esther, the daughter of Abihail the uncle of Mordecai, who had taken her for his daughter, was come to go in unto the king, she required nothing but what Hegai the king's chamberlain, the keeper of the women, appointed. And Esther obtained favour in the sight of all them that looked upon her.

16 So Esther was taken unto king Ahasuerus into his house royal in the tenth month, which is the month Tebeth, in the seventh year of his reign.

17 And the king loved Esther above all the women, and she obtained grace and favour in his sight more than all the virgins; so that he set the royal crown upon her head, and made her queen instead of Vashti.

18 Then the king made a great feast unto all his princes and his servants, even Esther's feast; and he made a release to the provinces, and gave gifts, according to the state of the king.

19 And when the virgins were gathered together the second time, then Mordecai sat in the king's gate.

20 Esther had not yet showed her kindred nor her people; as Mordecai had charged her: for Esther did the commandment of Mordecai, like as when she was brought up with him.

21 In those days, while Mordecai sat in the king's gate, two of the king's chamberlains, Bigthan and Teresh, of those which kept the door, were wroth, and sought to lay hand on the king Ahasuerus.

22 And the thing was known to Mordecai, who told it unto Esther the queen; and Esther certified the king thereof in Mordecai's name.

23 And when inquisition was made of the matter, it was found out; therefore they were both hanged on a tree: and it was written in the book of the chronicles before the king.

Chapter 3 _____

1 After these things did king Ahasuerus promote Haman the son of Hammedatha the Agagite, and advanced him, and set his seat above all the princes that were with him.

2 And all the king's servants, that were in the king's gate, bowed, and reverenced Haman: for the king had so commanded concerning him. But Mordecai bowed not, nor did him reverence.

3 Then the king's servants, which were in the king's gate, said unto Mordecai, Why transgressest thou the king's commandment?

4 Now it came to pass, when they spake daily unto him, and he hearkened not unto them, that they told Haman, to see whether Mordecai's matters would stand: for he had told them that he was a Jew.

5 And when Haman saw that Mordecai bowed not, nor did him reverence, then was Haman full of wrath.

6 And he thought scorn to lay hands on Mordecai alone; for they had showed him the people of Mordecai: wherefore Haman sought to destroy all the Jews that were throughout the whole kingdom of Ahasuerus, even the people of Mordecai.

7 In the first month, that is, the month Nisan, in the twelfth year of king Ahasuerus, they cast Pur, that is, the lot, before Haman from day to day, and from month to month, to the twelfth month, that is, the month Adar.

8 And Haman said unto king Ahasuerus, There is a certain people scattered abroad and dispersed among the people in all the provinces of thy kingdom; and their laws are diverse from all people; neither keep they the king's laws: therefore it is not for the king's profit to suffer them.

9 If it please the king, let it be written that they may be destroyed: and I will pay ten thousand talents of silver to the hands of those that have the charge of the business, to bring it into the king's treasuries.

10 And the king took his ring from his hand, and gave it unto Haman the son of Hammedatha the Agagite, the Jews' enemy.

11 And the king said unto Haman, The silver is given to thee, the people also, to do with them as it seemeth good to thee.

12 Then were the king's scribes called on the thirteenth day of the first month, and there was written according to all that Haman had commanded unto the king's lieutenants, and to the governors that were over every province, and to the rulers of every people of every province according to the writing thereof, and to every people after their language; in the name of king Ahasuerus was it written, and sealed with the king's ring.

13 And the letters were sent by posts into all the king's provinces, to destroy, to kill, and to cause to perish, all Jews, both young and old, little children and women, in one day, even upon the thirteenth day of the twelfth month, which is the month Adar, and to take the spoil of them for a prey.

14 The copy of the writing for a commandment to be given in every province was published unto all people, that they should be ready against that day.

15 The posts went out, being hastened by the king's commandment, and the decree was given in Shushan the palace. And the king and Haman sat down to drink; but the city Shushan was perplexed.

Chapter 4 _____

1 When Mordecai perceived all that was done, Mordecai rent his clothes, and put on sackcloth with ashes, and went out into the midst of the city, and cried with a loud and a bitter cry;

2 And came even before the king's gate: for none might enter into the king's gate clothed with sackcloth.

3 And in every province, whithersoever the king's commandment and his decree came, there was great mourning among the Jews, and fasting, and weeping, and wailing; and many lay in sackcloth and ashes.

4 So Esther's maids and her chamberlains came and told it her. Then was the queen exceedingly grieved; and she sent raiment to clothe Mordecai, and to take away his sackcloth from him: but he received it not.

5 Then called Esther for Hatach, one of the king's chamberlains, whom he had appointed to attend upon her, and gave him a commandment to Mordecai, to know what it was, and why it was.

6 So Hatach went forth to Mordecai unto the street of the city, which was before the king's gate.

7 And Mordecai told him of all that had happened unto him, and of the sum of the money that Haman had promised to pay to the king's treasuries for the Jews, to destroy them.

8 Also he gave him the copy of the writing of the decree that was given at Shushan to destroy them, to show it unto Esther, and to declare it unto her, and to charge her that she should go in unto the king, to make supplication unto him, and to make request before him for her people.

9 And Hatach came and told Esther the words of Mordecai.

10 Again Esther spake unto Hatach, and gave him commandment unto Mordecai;

11 All the king's servants, and the people of the king's provinces, do know, that whosoever, whether man or woman, shall come unto the king into the inner court, who is not called, there is one law of his to put him to death, except such to whom the king shall hold out the golden sceptre, that he may live: but I have not been called to come in unto the king these thirty days.

12 And they told to Mordecai Esther's words.

13 Then Mordecai commanded to answer Esther, Think not with thyself that thou shalt escape in the king's house, more than all the Jews.

14 For if thou altogether holdest thy peace at this time, then shall there enlargement and deliverance arise to the Jews from another place; but thou and thy father's house shall be destroyed: and who knoweth whether thou art come to the kingdom for such a time as this?

15 Then Esther bade them return Mordecai this answer,

16 Go, gather together all the Jews that are present in Shushan, and fast ye for me, and neither eat nor drink three days, night or day: I also and my maidens will fast likewise; and so will I go in unto the king, which is not according to the law: and if I perish, I perish.

17 So Mordecai went his way, and did according to all that Esther had commanded him.

Chapter 5 _____

1 Now it came to pass on the third day, that Esther put on her royal apparel, and stood in the inner court of the king's house, over against the king's house: and the king sat upon his royal throne in the royal house, over against the gate of the house.

2 And it was so, when the king saw Esther the queen standing in the court, that she obtained favour in his sight: and the king held out to Esther the golden sceptre that was in his hand. So Esther drew near, and touched the top of the sceptre.

3 Then said the king unto her, What wilt thou, queen Esther? and what is thy request? it shall be even given thee to the half of the kingdom.

4 And Esther answered, If it seem good unto the king, let the king and Haman come this day unto the banquet that I have prepared for him.

5 Then the king said, Cause Haman to make haste, that he may do as Esther hath said. So the king and Haman came to the banquet that Esther had prepared.

6 And the king said unto Esther at the banquet of wine, What is thy petition? and it shall be granted thee: and what is thy request? even to the half of the kingdom it shall be performed.

7 Then answered Esther, and said, My petition and my request is;

8 If I have found favour in the sight of the king, and if it please the king to grant my petition, and to perform my request, let the king and Haman come to the banquet that I shall prepare for them, and I will do to morrow as the king hath said.

9 Then went Haman forth that day joyful and with a glad heart: but when Haman saw Mordecai in the king's gate, that he stood not up, nor moved for him, he was full of indignation against Mordecai.

10 Nevertheless Haman refrained himself: and when he came home, he sent and called for his friends, and Zeresh his wife.

11 And Haman told them of the glory of his riches, and the multitude of his children, and all the things wherein the king had promoted him, and how he had advanced him above the princes and servants of the king.

12 Haman said moreover, Yea, Esther the queen did let no man come in with the king unto the banquet that she had prepared but myself; and to morrow am I invited unto her also with the king.

13 Yet all this availeth me nothing, so long as I see Mordecai the Jew sitting at the king's gate.

14 Then said Zeresh his wife and all his friends unto him, Let a gallows be made of fifty cubits high, and to morrow speak thou unto the king that Mordecai may be hanged thereon: then go thou in merrily with the king unto the banquet. And the thing pleased Haman; and he caused the gallows to be made.

Chapter 6

1 On that night could not the king sleep, and he commanded to bring the book of records of the chronicles; and they were read before the king.

2 And it was found written, that Mordecai had told of Bigthana and Teresh, two of the king's chamberlains, the keepers of the door, who sought to lay hand on the king Ahasuerus.

3 And the king said, What honour and dignity hath been done to Mordecai for this? Then said the king's servants that ministered unto him, There is nothing done for him.

4 And the king said, Who is in the court? Now Haman was come into the outward court of the king's house, to speak unto the king to hang Mordecai on the gallows that he had prepared for him.

5 And the king's servants said unto him, Behold, Haman standeth in the court. And the king said, Let him come in.

6 So Haman came in. And the king said unto him, What shall be done unto the man whom the king delighteth to honour? Now Haman thought in his heart, To whom would the king delight to do honour more than to myself?

7 And Haman answered the king, For the man whom the king delighteth to honour,

8 Let the royal apparel be brought which the king useth to wear, and the horse that the king rideth upon, and the crown royal which is set upon his head:

9 And let this apparel and horse be delivered to the hand of one of the king's most noble princes, that they may array the man withal whom the king delighteth to honour, and bring him on horseback through the street of the city, and proclaim before him, Thus shall it be done to the man whom the king delighteth to honour.

10 Then the king said to Haman, Make haste, and take the apparel and the horse, as thou hast said, and do even so to Mordecai the Jew, that sitteth at the king's gate: let nothing fail of all that thou hast spoken.

11 Then took Haman the apparel and the horse, and arrayed Mordecai, and brought him on horseback through the street of the city, and proclaimed before him, Thus shall it be done unto the man whom the king delighteth to honour.

12 And Mordecai came again to the king's gate. But Haman hasted to his house mourning, and having his head covered.

13 And Haman told Zeresh his wife and all his friends every thing that had befallen him. Then said his wise men and Zeresh his wife unto him, If Mordecai be of the seed of the Jews, before whom thou hast begun to fall, thou shalt not prevail against him, but shalt surely fall before him.

14 And while they were yet talking with him, came the king's chamberlains, and hasted to bring Haman unto the banquet that Esther had prepared.

Chapter 7 _____

1 So the king and Haman came to banquet with Esther the queen.

2 And the king said again unto Esther on the second day at the banquet of wine, What is thy petition, queen Esther? and it shall be granted thee: and what is thy request? and it shall be performed, even to the half of the kingdom.

3 Then Esther the queen answered and said, If I have found favour in thy sight, O king, and if it please the king, let my life be given me at my petition, and my people at my request:

4 For we are sold, I and my people, to be destroyed, to be slain, and to perish. But if we had been sold for bondmen and bondwomen, I had held my tongue, although the enemy could not countervail the king's damage.

5 Then the king Ahasuerus answered and said unto Esther the queen, Who is he, and where is he, that durst presume in his heart to do so?

6 And Esther said, The adversary and enemy is this wicked Haman. Then Haman was afraid before the king and the queen.

7 And the king arising from the banquet of wine in his wrath went into the palace garden: and Haman stood up to make request for his life to Esther the queen; for he saw that there was evil determined against him by the king.

8 Then the king returned out of the palace garden into the place of the banquet of wine; and Haman was fallen upon the bed whereon Esther was. Then said the king, Will he force the queen also before me in the house? As the word went out of the king's mouth, they covered Haman's face.

9 And Harbonah, one of the chamberlains, said before the king, Behold also, the gallows fifty cubits high, which Haman had made for Mordecai, who had spoken good for the king, standeth in the house of Haman. Then the king said, Hang him thereon.

10 So they hanged Haman on the gallows that he had prepared for Mordecai. Then was the king's wrath pacified.

Chapter 8 _____

1 On that day did the king Ahasuerus give the house of Haman the Jews' enemy unto Esther the queen. And Mordecai came before the king; for Esther had told what he was unto her.

2 And the king took off his ring, which he had taken from Haman, and gave it unto Mordecai. And Esther set Mordecai over the house of Haman.

3 And Esther spake yet again before the king, and fell down at his feet, and besought him with tears to put away the mischief of Haman the Agagite, and his device that he had devised against the Jews.

4 Then the king held out the golden sceptre toward Esther. So Esther arose, and stood before the king,

5 And said, If it please the king, and if I have found favour in his sight, and the thing seem right before the king, and I be pleasing in his eyes, let it be written to reverse the letters devised by Haman the son of Hammedatha the Agagite, which he wrote to destroy the Jews which are in all the king's provinces:

6 For how can I endure to see the evil that shall come unto my people? or how can I endure to see the destruction of my kindred?

7 Then the king Ahasuerus said unto Esther the queen and to Mordecai the Jew, Behold, I have given Esther the house of Haman, and him they have hanged upon the gallows, because he laid his hand upon the Jews.

8 Write ye also for the Jews, as it liketh you, in the king's name, and seal it with the king's ring: for the writing which is written in the king's name, and sealed with the king's ring, may no man reverse.

9 Then were the king's scribes called at that time in the third month, that is, the month Sivan, on the three and twentieth day thereof; and it was written according to all that Mordecai commanded unto the Jews, and to the lieutenants, and the deputies and rulers of the provinces which are from India unto Ethiopia, an hundred twenty and seven provinces, unto every province according to the writing thereof, and unto every people after their language, and to the Jews according to their writing, and according to their language.

10 And he wrote in the king Ahasuerus' name, and sealed it with the king's ring, and sent letters by posts on horseback, and riders on mules, camels, and young dromedaries:

11 Wherein the king granted the Jews which were in every city to gather themselves together, and to stand for their life, to destroy, to slay, and to cause to perish, all the power of the people and province that would assault them, both little ones and women, and to take the spoil of them for a prey,

12 Upon one day in all the provinces of king Ahasuerus, namely, upon the thirteenth day of the twelfth month, which is the month Adar.

13 The copy of the writing for a commandment to be given in every province was published unto all people, and that the Jews should be ready against that day to avenge themselves on their enemies.

14 So the posts that rode upon mules and camels went out, being hastened and pressed on by the king's commandment. And the decree was given at Shushan the palace.

15 And Mordecai went out from the presence of the king in royal apparel of blue and white, and with a great crown of gold, and with a garment of fine linen and purple: and the city of Shushan rejoiced and was glad.

16 The Jews had light, and gladness, and joy, and honour.

17 And in every province, and in every city, whithersoever the king's commandment and his decree came, the Jews had joy and gladness, a feast and a good day. And many of the people of the land became Jews; for the fear of the Jews fell upon them.

Chapter 9 _____

1 Now in the twelfth month, that is, the month Adar, on the thirteenth day of the same, when the king's commandment and his decree drew near to be put in execution, in the day that the enemies of the Jews hoped to have power over them, (though it was turned to the contrary, that the Jews had rule over them that hated them;)

2 The Jews gathered themselves together in their cities throughout all the provinces of the king Ahasuerus, to lay hand on such as sought their hurt: and no man could withstand them; for the fear of them fell upon all people.

3 And all the rulers of the provinces, and the lieutenants, and the deputies, and officers of the king, helped the Jews; because the fear of Mordecai fell upon them.

4 For Mordecai was great in the king's house, and his fame went out throughout all the provinces: for this man Mordecai waxed greater and greater.

5 Thus the Jews smote all their enemies with the stroke of the sword, and slaughter, and destruction, and did what they would unto those that hated them.

6 And in Shushan the palace the Jews slew and destroyed five hundred men.

7 And Parshandatha, and Dalphon, and Aspatha,

8 And Poratha, and Adalia, and Aridatha,

9 And Parmashta, and Arisai, and Aridai, and Vajezatha,

10 The ten sons of Haman the son of Hammedatha, the enemy of the Jews, slew they; but on the spoil laid they not their hand.

11 On that day the number of those that were slain in Shushan the palace was brought before the king.

12 And the king said unto Esther the queen, The Jews have slain and destroyed five hundred men in Shushan the palace, and the ten sons of Haman; what have they done in the rest of the king's provinces? now what is thy petition? and it shall be granted thee: or what is thy request further? and it shall be done.

13 Then said Esther, If it please the king, let it be granted to the Jews which are in Shushan to do to morrow also according unto this day's decree, and let Haman's ten sons be hanged upon the gallows.

14 And the king commanded it so to be done: and the decree was given at Shushan; and they hanged Haman's ten sons.

15 For the Jews that were in Shushan gathered themselves together on the fourteenth day also of the month Adar, and slew three hundred men at Shushan; but on the prey they laid not their hand.

16 But the other Jews that were in the king's provinces gathered themselves together, and stood for their lives, and had rest from their enemies, and slew of their foes seventy and five thousand, but they laid not their hands on the prey,

17 On the thirteenth day of the month Adar; and on the fourteenth day of the same rested they, and made it a day of feasting and gladness.

18 But the Jews that were at Shushan assembled together on the thirteenth day thereof, and on the fourteenth thereof; and on the fifteenth day of the same they rested, and made it a day of feasting and gladness.

19 Therefore the Jews of the villages, that dwelt in the unwalled towns, made the fourteenth day of the month Adar a day of gladness and feasting, and a good day, and of sending portions one to another.

20 And Mordecai wrote these things, and sent letters unto all the Jews that were in all the provinces of the king Ahasuerus, both nigh and far,

21 To stablish this among them, that they should keep the fourteenth day of the month Adar, and the fifteenth day of the same, yearly,

22 As the days wherein the Jews rested from their enemies, and the month which was turned unto them from sorrow to joy, and from mourning into a good day: that they should make them days of feasting and joy, and of sending portions one to another, and gifts to the poor.

23 And the Jews undertook to do as they had begun, and as Mordecai had written unto them;

24 Because Haman the son of Hammedatha, the Agagite, the enemy of all the Jews, had devised against the Jews to destroy them, and had cast Pur, that is, the lot, to consume them, and to destroy them;

25 But when Esther came before the king, he commanded by letters that his wicked device, which he devised against the Jews, should return upon his own head, and that he and his sons should be hanged on the gallows.

26 Wherefore they called these days Purim after the name of Pur. Therefore for all the words of this letter, and of that which they had seen concerning this matter, and which had come unto them,

27 The Jews ordained, and took upon them, and upon their seed, and upon all such as joined themselves unto them, so as it should not fail, that they would keep these two days according to their writing, and according to their appointed time every year;

28 And that these days should be remembered and kept throughout every generation, every family, every province, and every city; and that these days of Purim should not fail from among the Jews, nor the memorial of them perish from their seed.

29 Then Esther the queen, the daughter of Abihail, and Mordecai the Jew, wrote with all authority, to confirm this second letter of Purim.

30 And he sent the letters unto all the Jews, to the hundred twenty and seven provinces of the kingdom of Ahasuerus, with words of peace and truth,

31 To confirm these days of Purim in their times appointed, according as Mordecai the Jew and Esther the queen had enjoined them, and as they had decreed for themselves and for their seed, the matters of the fastings and their cry.

32 And the decree of Esther confirmed these matters of Purim; and it was written in the book.

Chapter 10 _____

1 And the king Ahasuerus laid a tribute upon the land, and upon the isles of the sea.

2 And all the acts of his power and of his might, and the declaration of the greatness of Mordecai, whereunto the king advanced him, are they not written in the book of the chronicles of the kings of Media and Persia?

3 For Mordecai the Jew was next unto king Ahasuerus, and great among the Jews, and accepted of the multitude of his brethren, seeking the wealth of his people, and speaking peace to all his seed.

Study No. 7

Beauty on the Move

"Even as Sara obeyed Abraham,
calling him lord: whose daughters ye are,
as long as ye do well,
and are not afraid with any amazement."

(1 Peter 3:6)

Even as an older woman, Sarah was so beautiful that her husband knew she would attract the attention of kings in the foreign lands they traversed. She is also praised in the New Testament as an example of fearless submission and God-honoring faith.

This study will outline the basics of a **character study**, as we examine Sarah's life and learn about the inner beauty of this outwardly beautiful woman.

1. ☆ Use a concordance, Bible dictionary, or Bible encyclopedia to help you find all the references to Sarai and Sarah in the Bible. Record these references below.

   _____

   _____

   _____

   _____

   _____

2. Note also the verses in Hebrews 11 that refer to Abraham and list these below.

   _____

   _____

3. Read the passages and their surrounding verses, carefully observing and recording any information you find for each of the categories listed below:

   a. Meaning of her name

   _____

   _____

b. Her family and ancestry

_____

_____

c. The times in which she lived

_____

_____

_____

d. Where she lived (Locate these areas on a map in a Bible or Bible atlas, if possible.)

_____

_____

_____

e. The activities and events of her life

_____

_____

_____

_____

_____

_____

f. Her acts of obedience

_____

_____

_____

_____

_____

_____

g. The temptations and challenges she faced

_____

_____

_____

_____

h. Her shortcomings and apparent mistakes

_____

_____

_____

_____

_____

i. The effect of her life on others

_____

_____

_____

j. The way she died and its impact on others

_____

_____

4. Review your notes and write a short biographical sketch of Sarah.

_____

_____

_____

_____

_____

_____

_____

_____

_____

_____

5. Note any questions you have about the life of Sarah. List any events in her life that you do not understand or Scripture passages that are unclear to you.

_____

_____

_____

_____

_____

_____

6. Seek to answer the above questions with the help of your parents, pastor, and commentaries and other reference books.

_____

_____

_____

_____

_____

_____

7. List 5 descriptive words that summarize Sarah's character.

_____

_____

8. What lessons can you learn from the life of Sarah?

_____

_____

_____

_____

_____

9. In what areas is God calling you to change after studying the life of Sarah? Outline a specific plan that will, with God's help, lead to these changes.

_____

_____

_____

_____

_____

_____

For further study:

- I Peter 3:6 says that we are Sarah's daughters when we choose to obey and "are not afraid with any amazement." Use your concordance to study Scripture passages that tell us to "fear not." What do you learn from these passages that will help you fearlessly obey as Sarah did?

- Using the method outlined in Study No. 3, "Beauty and the Pit," do a topical study of the subject "trust." What do you learn that will help you more obediently trust God in all the circumstances of your life?

- Make a list of all God's promises as you read through the entire Bible. Note each reference and promise. Categorize these promises in a form that you can review when you need encouragement to trust God in all things.

- Study Hebrews 11. What is faith? Study the lives of each example of faith mentioned in the chapter.

Study No. 8

Beauty in the Works

"In like manner also,
that women adorn themselves in modest apparel,
with shamefacedness and sobriety;
not with broided hair, or gold, or pearls, or costly array;
But (which becometh women professing godliness)
with good works."

(1 Timothy 2:9-10)

Godly beauty is not passive. It is a condition of the soul that quietly, diligently expresses itself through actions! In this study we will examine what God says about a godly woman's true adornment. On what does a woman's true beauty depend?

1 Timothy 2:9-10 speaks of a godly woman's **adorning**. The Greek word for **adorning** is **kosmeo**, which means **to put in proper order** or **to decorate**. It is also translated **garnish** and **trim**. It comes from the word **kosmos**, which means **orderly arrangement**.

1. Copy in your own handwriting the two verses listed above.

   _____

   _____

   _____

   _____

   _____

2. With a colored pencil or felt pen, mark all the words in your copied verses that describe how a woman should seek to adorn or beautify herself.

3. With another color of marker, mark the words that tell us what a woman should **not** rely on for beauty.

4. These verses list four aspects of a godly woman's beauty:

   a. **Modest apparel:** The Greek word for **modest** is **kosmios**, which comes from **kosmos**, the exact same word that is used for **adorning**. A woman's modest apparel is **put in proper order** or **orderly**. A godly woman's spirit is reflected in her outward clothing and appearance.

b. **Shamefacedness:** The Greek word is **aidos** and describes an attitude of **downcast eyes** or **bashfulness**. It describes a woman's posture toward men, and a person's awe or godly fear of God. A godly woman's spirit is reflected in her eyes.

c. **Sobriety:** The Greek word is **sophrosune** which means **soundness of mind**. The word speaks of sanity and self-control. A godly woman's spirit is reflected in the controlled expression of her thoughts and emotions.

d. **Good works:** The Greek word translated as **good** is **agathos** which means **benefit**. The word for **works** is **ergon**. This noun comes from a verb which means "**to work, toil, as an effort or occupation**." A godly woman's spirit is reflected in the way she treats other people and in the way she uses her time and energy.

Each of these elements of godly beauty merits our attention. The godly woman is modest in attitude, action, and appearance. She, with God's help, keeps her thoughts and emotions under control. Her life is characterized by acts of love and service. For the purpose of this study we will be focusing on the good works that are part of a godly woman's true beauty.

5. Use a concordance to locate verses about **good works**. Look under the word **good**. Although it has a very long list of entries, you should be able to skim the list fairly quickly, only noting the references for verses that also include the words **work**, **works**, or **deeds**. (If your family has any Bible software on a computer, this task will be much easier because you can let the program search on the phrase **good works**.)

6. If you have a **Nave's Topical Bible** you can also look up the word **works** in it. Skim all the verses, identifying those that refer to good works or good deeds.

7. In the space below, list the references of each verse you want to read. Put one reference on each line. Leave space to record your observations for each verse.

_____

_____

_____

_____

_____

_____

_____

_____

_____

_____

_____

_____

_____

_____

_____

_____

_____

_____

_____

_____

8. Read each of the verses you have listed, along with the verses that precede and follow them. On the same line as the verse reference, note what you learn about good works in each passage.

9. After you have studied each passage, review your notes and organize them under the following topics:

    a. What are good works?

    _____

    _____

    _____

    _____

    _____

    _____

b. What good works are listed?

_____

_____

_____

_____

_____

c. Who are the recipients of good works?

_____

_____

_____

_____

_____

d. What Biblical characters are described as doers of good works? What did they do? How did their beneficiaries respond?

_____

_____

_____

_____

_____

e. How are we equipped for good works?

_____

_____

_____

_____

f. What should be our motivation in doing good works?

_____

_____

_____

_____

_____

g. What are the rewards of doing good works?

_____

_____

_____

_____

_____

10. Read 2 Timothy 2:20-21. What does the word **sanctified** mean?

_____

_____

11. What dishes do you use for very special occasions in your home? Does your mother have special china she only uses for holidays? Does she have heirloom dishes or glassware that she only displays and does not use? What would she do if you used one of her special dishes to feed the dog? What if your brother used one of the dishes for holding the worms he gathered for his next fishing trip? Why?

_____

_____

_____

12. How are we, as Christians, like those special dishes? For what purpose has God set us apart?

_____

_____

13. Read Ephesians 2:8-10. Do we earn our salvation by good works? What are we created for in Christ Jesus?

_____

_____

14. Read James 2:26. What does it say about faith and its relationship to works?

_____

_____

15. Read 1 Corinthians 13. What trait needs to be present in a person's life for her good works to be profitable?

_____

16. List the main characteristics of this trait as it is described in 1 Corinthians 13:4-8.

_____

_____

_____

17. How many of these characteristics are present in your life?

_____

_____

18. In what areas of love do you need to grow?

_____

_____

19. List at least 4 specific goals and actions that you will commit to in order to "put on" love. Be specific. What will you do? Who will you do it for? When will you do it?

_____

_____

_____

_____

20. Make a list of twenty different good works that you can do now, in your youth. Think of what you can do for your parents, your grandparents, your siblings, your friends, your neighbors, elderly people, other young people in your church or school, and others who have less than you do.

_____

_____

_____

_____

_____

_____

_____

_____

_____

_____

_____

_____

_____

_____

_____

_____

_____

_____

21. Commit to performing, as unto Jesus, at least one of these good works each week.

For Further Study:

- Read Proverbs 31:10-31. What is the visible demonstration of the virtuous woman's fear of the Lord? What will "praise her in the gates?" Verse 31 says that the virtuous woman's works will praise her in the gates. Study the passage and list the good works that are described.

- Use a concordance to help you study the meaning of **shamefacedness** and **sobriety**. What does the Bible say about these attitudes of spirit?

- Study the topic of **clothing** in the Bible. How is God clothed? How is creation clothed? How are believers clothed? What is the purpose of clothing?

- Study the relationship between faith and works. What is the role of works in the Christian life?

Study No. 9
Beauty and the Fool

"Now the name of the man was Nabal;
and the name of his wife Abigail:
and she was a woman of good understanding,
and of a beautiful countenance. . .
'And blessed be thy advice, and blessed be thou,
which has kept me this day from
coming to shed blood,
and from avenging myself with my own hand.' "

(1 Samuel 25:3a and 33)

Beauty with Discretion

1. Abigail is described by God as a woman of "beautiful countenance." The Hebrew word for **beautiful** in this verse is **yaphah**. It is the same word that is translated **fair** in Proverbs 11:22, our verse about the fair woman who is without discretion.

   God also tells us that Abigail was a "woman of good understanding." The Hebrew word for **understanding** is **sekel**. It is defined as "intelligence." It comes from the word **sakal**, which means "to be circumspect."

   Look up the word "circumspect" in the dictionary. What does it mean?

   _____

   _____

   _____

2. **Sekel** is also translated into the English as **discretion, knowledge, policy, prudence, sense, wisdom**, and **wise**.

   Read the following verses. Each one uses the word **sekel**. Summarize each verse. What does it say about "understanding?" From where does this understanding come?

   a. 1 Chronicles 22:12 (wisdom)

   _____

   b. Nehemiah 8:8 (sense)

   _____

80

c. Job 17:4 (understanding)

_____

d. Psalm 111:10 (understanding)

_____

e. Proverbs 3:4 (understanding)

_____

f. Proverbs 16:22 (understanding)

_____

g. Proverbs 19:11 (discretion)

_____

h. Proverbs 23:9 (wisdom)

_____

3. Read 1 Samuel 25:33. What and whom does David say are blessed?

_____

In **The New American Standard Bible**, David says to Abigail, "Blessed be your discernment." The Hebrew word that has been translated as "discernment" in the NASB and as "advice" in the King James Version is the same original Hebrew word that is translated "discretion" in Proverbs 11:22. "As a jewel of gold in a swine's snout, so is a fair woman which is without **discretion**."

Abigail is a **fair woman with discretion**. She is the opposite of the pig with the gold ring in its nose. She is a woman who is beautiful but **does** have wisdom and understanding, unlike the indiscreet woman in Proverbs 11:22. Let's see how she compares!

A Description of the Fool

4. Read 1 Samuel 25. Read the chapter a second time and use a highlighter or colored pencil to mark every word or phrase that is used to describe Nabal. List those descriptive words and phrases below.

a. _____

b. _____

c. _____

d. _____

e. _____

f. _____

g. _____

h. _____

i. _____

j. _____

k. _____

5. Read 1 Samuel 25:10-11. How does Nabal respond to the request of David's men for food?

_____

_____

6. How many times does Nabal use the words "I" and "**my**" in these verses? _____

7. Read Luke 12:18-20. What do Nabal and the rich man in this parable have in common? What happens to the rich man? What happens to Nabal?

_____

_____

8. Read Proverbs 11:28. How does the truth of this Proverb relate to the accounts of these two rich men?

_____

_____

9. Read 1 Samuel 17. What did David, in God's name and strength, do in this chapter?

_____

_____

_____

10. Read 1 Samuel 18:5-7 and 16. How did the people respond to David and his accomplishments?

_____

_____

_____

11. Reread 1 Samuel 25:10-11. Do you think Nabal really doesn't know who David is? Why would he respond in this way if he **does** know who David is?

_____

_____

_____

The Beauty of Careful Listening

12. Read 1 Samuel 25:28-30. What does Abigail know about David and his future? Does she appear to believe all that she has heard about David?

_____

_____

_____

13. Read 1 Samuel 25:14-17.

What is the message of the servant?

_____

What does he appeal to Abigail to do?

_____

Why does he want her to do this?

_____

The Beauty of a Prudent Response

14. Read 1 Samuel 25:18-19. What is Abigail's plan?

_____

_____

_____

15. Note what David asked of Nabal in verse 8 and what Abigail prepared to take to him in verse 18. How do they compare? Why do you think Abigail did this?

_____

_____

_____

16. Read 1 Samuel 25:20-22. What is David's plan?

_____

_____

The Beauty of a Respectful Appeal

17. In verses 23 through 31, carefully read Abigail's appeal to David:

What did Abigail do when she saw David? List each action.

_____

_____

_____

_____

_____

_____

Use a colored pencil to mark each time Abigail refers to David as "my lord." How many times in this brief conversation does she address him in this way? _____

Use another colored pencil to highlight each time Abigail refers to herself as "thine handmaid." How many times does she use this term of humility? _____

What do these words communicate about Abigail's attitude as she appeals to David? Is her attitude different than that of her husband?

_____

_____

_____

18. In verses 17 and 25 Nabal is referred to as a "son of Belial" by his servant and a "man of Belial" by his wife. Is Abigail speaking disrespectfully of her husband? Read the following verses that refer to others as sons or children of Belial. Identify these people and their actions.

    a. 1 Samuel 2:12 _____

    b. 2 Samuel 20:1 _____

    c. 1 Kings 21:10 _____

    d. What do these people all have in common? _____

    _____

19. Read 2 Corinthians 6:15. What do you learn about Belial in this passage? To whom is he contrasted? (What concord has Christ with Belial, and believer with infidel?)

_____

_____

Abigail says of her husband that "**Nabal** is his name, and **folly** (nebalah, in Hebrew) is with him."

Strong's Exhaustive Concordance defines the meaning of **Nabal** as "dolt." Noah Webster's **1828 American Dictionary of the English Language** defines a dolt as "a heavy, stupid fellow; a blockhead; a thick-skull." It traces the word to origins that mean "to wander" or "to sleep or be drowsy." This is the name of Abigail's husband, perhaps a nickname that he earned from his actions and personality.

The word for **folly** (**nebalah**) comes from the same Hebrew root, and means "foolishness" or "wickedness." The word is used to describe the sinful actions of men and women who openly rebelled against God and His law.

The word **folly** (**nebalah**) is used to described the actions of:

- Amnon, who raped his sister Tamar (2 Samuel 13:12)
- Achan, who stole forbidden spoil when Israel conquered Jericho (Joshua 7:15)
- "Sons of Belial" who sought to rape the Levite in Gibeah (Judges 19:23)
- An unmarried woman who was not a virgin (Deuteronomy 22:21)

This is a different word than the Hebrew word **ivveleth** that is translated as "folly" in the book of Proverbs. That word means "silliness." It is contrasted to the prudence or wisdom that is able to apply the principles of God's Word to life.

Abigail is not arrogantly calling her husband a stupid idiot. She is acknowledging that he is a rebellious man who does not fear God. Godly actions should not be expected of him.

The Beauty of Wise Counsel

20. Read I Samuel 25:26. From what does she say the Lord has restrained David?

_____

_____

21. Notice what Abigail says at the end of verse 26, "Now let thine enemies, and they that seek evil to my lord, be as Nabal." Does she expect Nabal to live through his sinful action of insulting David, the Lord's anointed? _____

22. In verses 28-31 Abigail reminds David of God's promises, and makes several statements about David, his future, and the future of his enemies. List each statement below:

_____

_____

_____

_____

_____

23. Read Abigail's appeal in verse 31. For what sins does she not want David's heart to be troubled?

_____

_____

24. In verses 32-35, how does David respond to Abigail's appeal?

Blessed be _____

Blessed be _____

Blessed be _____

25. Who does David say restrained him from carrying out his plan?

_____

_____

26. Read 1 Samuel 24:1-12. What did David do when given the opportunity to avenge himself of Saul's wrongdoings?

_____

_____

_____

27. What did David say in verse 12? Would this same truth also apply to his circumstances with Nabal? _____

28. Read 1 Samuel 25:35. How did David respond to Abigail's appeal?

_____

_____

29. Read 1 Samuel 25:36. What was Nabal doing while David was preparing to kill him and his household?

_____

_____

30. Abigail chose to not tell Nabal about her encounter with David until the next day. Read the following Proverbs. What do they say?

    a. Proverbs 20:1

    _____

    _____

    b. Proverbs 23:29-30

    _____

    _____

    _____

31. Why do you think Abigail chose to wait?

_____

_____

32. According to 1 Samuel 25:37-38, what happened to Nabal?

_____

_____

33. Read 1 Samuel 25:39. How did David respond to the news of Nabal's death?

_____

_____

34. Read Deuteronomy 32:35. What does this verse say about vengeance? How does this apply to the story of Nabal?

_____

_____

35. Read Proverbs 19:29. How does the truth of this verse relate to the story of Nabal?

_____

_____

36. Read Proverbs 15:2. How is the truth of this Proverb illustrated in the story of Nabal and Abigail?

_____

_____

37. Proverbs 25:12 speaks of another ring of gold, but this one is not in a pig's nose. Read this verse and tell how it relates to the story of Abigail and David.

_____

_____

_____

38. Review the story of Abigail and your notes in this study. In what ways did Abigail show discretion?

_____

_____

_____

_____

_____

_____

39. ✶ In what similar ways can you show discretion in your own life? Think about relationships
with siblings, parents, friends, and neighbors. List specific actions you will take.

_____

_____

_____

_____

_____

_____

For further study:

- Study other appeals in Scripture. How does Esther's appeal to Ahasuerus compare to
  Abigail's appeal to David? Study Bathsheba's appeal to David in 1 Kings 1:11-31. How are
  these appeals alike? How are they different? What can you learn from them? What can you
  apply to your relationships with parents, teachers, and other authorities?

- How should we treat an angry person, or a person who treats us or others unjustly? Study
  the Bible to find the answer to this question.

Study No. 10

Beauty in the Gates

"Who can find a virtuous woman? for her price is far above rubies…
…Favour is deceitful, and beauty is vain:
but a woman that feareth the LORD, she shall be praised."

(Proverbs 31:10 and 30))

"And now, my daughter, fear not;
I will do to thee all that thou requirest:
for all the city of my people doth know that thou art a virtuous woman."

(Ruth 3:11)

The story of Ruth is a beautiful story of love and redemption. Ruth is the **one** woman in the Bible that is identified as a **virtuous** woman.

Boaz says in Ruth 3:11, "…for all the city of my people doth know that thou art a virtuous woman." The word that Boaz used to describe Ruth is the same word that is used in Proverbs 31 to describe the virtuous woman that every man should seek.

This same word is also used to describe brave and strong men of character, "mighty men of valor." Ruth could be called a "mighty woman of valor," and like the Proverbs 31 mighty woman of valor, she was praised in the gates. The people of the city knew that she was a virtuous woman. They knew from her **actions**.

1. Read the book of Ruth several times. If you desire, read the book in different translations each time. Write a brief summary of the story in the space below.

_____

_____

_____

_____

_____

_____

2. Read the story one more time and list on the next pages all of Ruth's actions. What did she do? (For example, Chapter 1, verse 7 says that Ruth traveled with Naomi and Orpah to return to Judah.) Be sure to also note what other people say about her.

Ruth's actions:

_____

_____

_____

_____

_____

_____

_____

_____

_____

_____

_____

_____

_____

_____

_____

_____

_____

_____

_____

_____

Ruth's actions (continued):

_____

_____

_____

_____

3. What did the people of Bethlehem know about Ruth?

_____

_____

_____

_____

4. Do you see any basic characteristics of Ruth demonstrated in her actions? What was she like?

_____

_____

_____

_____

5. Read Proverbs 31:10-31 below. Review the list of actions that you recorded while reading the story of Ruth. Ruth's actions and words demonstrated the virtuous character that people recognized in her. As you read the Proverbs passage one more time, write down Ruth's actions and words next to the verses that describe similar actions and attitudes in the virtuous woman.

10 Who can find a virtuous woman? for her price is far above rubies.

11 The heart of her husband doth safely trust in her, so that he shall have no need of spoil.

12 She will do him good and not evil all the days of her life.

13 She seeketh wool, and flax, and worketh willingly with her hands.

14 She is like the merchants' ships; she bringeth her food from afar.

15 She riseth also while it is yet night, and giveth meat to her household, and a portion to her maidens.

16 She considereth a field, and buyeth it: with the fruit of her hands she planteth a vineyard.

17 She girdeth her loins with strength, and strengtheneth her arms.

18 She perceiveth that her merchandise is good: her candle goeth not out by night.

19 She layeth her hands to the spindle, and her hands hold the distaff.

20 She stretcheth out her hand to the poor; yea, she reacheth forth her hands to the needy.

21 She is not afraid of the snow for her household: for all her household are clothed with scarlet.

22 She maketh herself coverings of tapestry; her clothing is silk and purple.

23 Her husband is known in the gates, when he sitteth among the elders of the land.

24 She maketh fine linen, and selleth it; and delivereth girdles unto the merchant.

25 Strength and honour are her clothing; and she shall rejoice in time to come.

26 She openeth her mouth with wisdom; and in her tongue is the law of kindness.

27 She looketh well to the ways of her household, and eateth not the bread of idleness.

28 Her children arise up, and call her blessed; her husband also, and he praiseth her.

29 Many daughters have done virtuously, but thou excellest them all.

30 Favour is deceitful, and beauty is vain: but a woman that feareth the LORD, she shall be praised.

31 Give her of the fruit of her hands; and let her own works praise her in the gates.

6. Read Ruth 1:16. Remember Ruth was a Moabite woman. She lived in a land of idol worshippers. She tells Naomi, "Your people shall be my people, and your God, my God." What is she declaring when she says this?

_____

_____

7. Read Ruth 4:17. How is Ruth related to King David?

_____

8. Reread Proverbs 31:30-31

30 Favour is deceitful, and beauty is vain: but a woman that feareth the LORD, she shall be praised.

31 Give her of the fruit of her hands; and let her own works praise her in the gates.

9. How does the life of Ruth demonstrate this truth from Scripture?

_____

_____

10. Are you known by your works? Can others tell, by your actions, that you fear God ? _____

11. What traits in Ruth's character are ones that you should emulate?

_____

_____

_____

_____

_____

12. ★ List specific actions that you, with God's help, will take to build the same character traits in your own life.

_____

_____

_____

_____

For further study:

- Use a concordance to help you study "the fear of the Lord." What promises are associated with fearing God? What actions demonstrate one's fear of the Lord? After you organize your findings, review Ruth's life again. How is her fear for God demonstrated in the book of Ruth? How is it demonstrated in your life?

- Study the lives of other men and women in the Bible who are described as fearing God. Use the character study method that is outlined in Study No. 7, "Beauty on the Move."

- Conduct a topical study on **wisdom**. What is wisdom? To what is it compared? How valuable is it? How can you relate your findings to what you have learned about a woman's true beauty?

Beauty in Review

God describes true beauty in His Word. We have studied the lives of beautiful women. We have studied what Scripture says about physical beauty and how it can be wasted or abused. While studying beauty, we have also learned how to study the Bible. In this brief lesson, we will review what we have learned.

1. Write a brief essay that summarizes God's definition of beauty. Consider the following questions while writing your essay:

   • What is discretion?

   • How does one gain discretion?

   • How can a girl or woman act like a pig?

   • In what ways can a woman display a lack of discretion and spiritual ugliness?

   • What actions and attitudes make a woman truly beautiful in God's eyes?

   • What is the beautiful woman's attitude toward others?

   • How does a beautiful and discreet woman treat men?

   • What is the beautiful woman's attitude toward authority?

   • What women in Scripture can we study as examples of godly beauty? What can we learn from them?

   _____

   _____

   _____

   _____

   _____

   _____

   _____

   _____

   _____

   _____

_____

_____

_____

_____

_____

_____

_____

_____

_____

_____

2. ✭ Think of a truly beautiful Christian woman that you know. Observe her and record your observations.

- How does she respond to God's Word?

- How does she interact with other people?

- How does she serve others?

- How does she treat her husband?

- How does she treat her children?

- How does she use her God-given talents?

- How does she deal with disagreements?

- How does she use her time?

- How does she dress?

- How does she look?

_____

_____

_____

_____

_____

_____

_____

_____

_____

_____

_____

_____

_____

3. ★ Is God calling you to become more beautiful in heart and soul? Are there specific areas in your life that you know, with the Holy Spirit's help, need to change? After seeking the guidance of God and your parents, outline a specific plan to help you grow in godly beauty. Then follow your plan!

_____

_____

_____

_____

_____

_____

_____

_____

_____

_____

_____

_____

_____

4. Explain how to perform a topical study in the Bible. How do you find out more about a specific topic in the Bible? What resources will help you? (See Study No. 8, "Beauty in the Words.")

_____

_____

_____

_____

5. Explain how to perform a character study in the Bible. How can you locate all the passages that tell about a specific person in the Bible? What observations should you make as you read about the person? (See Study No. 7, "Beauty on the Move.")

_____

_____

_____

_____

_____

6. When studying a book of the Bible, what six questions will help you to carefully observe what the passage says? (See Study No. 6, "Beauty and the Feast.")

_____

_____

_____

_____

7. To a friend or sibling, explain how to use a concordance to locate the original word used in a passage of Scripture. How do you find out what Hebrew or Greek word was used in the passage? How do you find out what the word means? How can you find other verses that use the same original Hebrew or Greek word? (See Study No. 4, "Beauty and the Drip.")

8. **Future study topics.** As you continue to study God's Word you will think of many words, topics, passages, and people that you would like to study more. In the space below keep a record of other studies you would like to pursue. When you conclude one study you can refer to this list for ideas for your next study. Your parents may wish to add their suggestions to your list.

_____

_____

_____

_____

_____

_____

_____

_____

_____

_____

_____

_____

_____

_____

_____

_____

_____

_____

Questions for Young Men

Proverbs was written for young men. "My son, hear the instruction… My son, if thou wilt receive my words…My son, forget not my law…My son, let them not depart from thine eyes…My son, attend unto my wisdom…"

Proverbs 11:22 was written to young men. "As a jewel of gold in a swine's snout, so is a fair woman which is without discretion." Young men need to know about godly beauty, and they need to know how to recognize a woman who has no discretion!

Young men, as well as young ladies, need to learn about godly beauty from the Bible. The following questions are offered as alternatives for the young men who are doing the studies in this book. Many questions in each study will apply to both young ladies and young men. However, some are aimed directly to young ladies. These questions are marked with a star (★) in each study. If you are a young man doing these studies, you can refer to this chapter to find questions designed for you. Each question is listed under the study's title, with the number of the question it replaces in the original study.

Study No. 1, "Beauty and the Word"

15. Read Proverbs 1:1-9. What is the purpose of the Book of Proverbs? How does this relate to the discretion that young ladies should possess? How does it relate to the discretion that young men should possess?

_____

_____

_____

Study No. 2, "Beauty and the Pig"

29. Examine your own life.

   a. Do you have associations with young ladies who behave like pigs? In what ways do they demonstrate their lack of discretion?

   _____

   _____

   _____

   _____

   b. Read Proverbs 2:10-18 and Proverbs 5:1-5. What role does discretion play in your godly response to these young ladies?

   _____

_____

_____

_____

    c. Read Genesis 39:7-12. How did Joseph respond to a woman who had no discretion?

_____

_____

Study No. 3, "Beauty in the Pit"

3. Listed below are descriptive phrases from the book of Proverbs about the strange woman. Meditate on each phrase and answer each question. Also ask for your parents' opinions about each question. They may see you differently than you are able to see yourself.

    a. 7:5 **"flattereth with her words"** and 7:21 **"much fair speech," "flattering of her lips"**
   - Am I inappropriately impressed with verbal praise or open admiration of others?
   - Do I give inappropriate attention and favor to those who compliment or admire me?

    b. 7:10 **"with the attire of an harlot and subtil of heart"**
   - Do I accept responsibility to guard my eyes and thoughts relative to the dress and appearance of young ladies?
   - Do I focus on a young lady's face and character?
   - Do I treat young ladies as sisters and as the future wives of others?
   - Do I respond to young ladies in a way that would encourage them to dress and behave immodestly?

    c. 7:11 **"loud"**
   - Do I give attention to young ladies who make loud and silly remarks in the company of others?
   - Do I discourage or encourage young ladies who take too much initiative in relating to me and other young men in a way that is too familiar?

    d. 7:11 **"stubborn"**
   - Am I protecting myself from stubborn young ladies by submitting to the leadership of my parents, teachers, and authorities?
   - Do my words and actions encourage young ladies to be submissive to the authorities in their lives?

    e. 7:11 **"her feet abide not in her house"**
   - Do I appreciate young ladies who enjoy serving others in their homes?

    f. 7:13 **"an impudent face"** and 6:25 **"take thee with her eyelids"**

- Am I overly impressed or influenced by the looks and words of young ladies?
- Do I allow myself to be manipulated by the words and gestures of young ladies?

g. 7:16 **"decked [her] bed with coverings of tapestry, with carved works, with fine linen of Egypt"** and 7:17 **"perfumed [her] bed with myrrh, aloes, and cinnamon"**
- Am I physically attracted to young ladies in ways that do not bring glory to God?
- Do I give attention to young ladies who place too much emphasis on makeup, perfumes, jewelry, and clothing?

h. 7:19 **"For the goodman is not at home, he is gone a long journey."**
- What do I do when I know a young lady's parents are not at home?
- What do I do when I am not under the direct oversight of my parents or other authority?

i. 7:22 **"He goeth after her straightway."**
- Do I make a "game" of flirting with foolish young ladies?
- Do I mistakenly believe that I am strong enough to resist the temptations that a foolish young lady can place before me?
- Am I committed to "fleeing" when presented with temptation from young ladies?

j. 2:17 **"Forsaketh the guide of her youth, and forgetteth the covenant of her God."**
- Do I encourage young ladies to step out from under the authority of Scripture and their parents?
- Am I behaving like a son of The King? Am I encouraging young ladies to behave like daughters of The King?

4. Skip this question.

6. Prayerfully review this entire lesson. Then list specific actions, attitudes and thoughts that you need to change to become a strong and godly man, protected from the foolish and seducing woman. Ask your parents for their opinions, as well.

_____

_____

_____

_____

_____

_____

_____

Study No. 5, "Beauty and the Drip"

D1. What is the Holy Spirit saying to you through your study of 1 Peter 2:13-3:9? Does your life reflect the kind of strong, quiet submission that Jesus demonstrated in His life? Are you compassionate and courteous? Are you willing to bless rather than returning evil for evil? In what areas do you need to change? Think about your relationship to the authorities in your life. Think about your attitudes and words toward your siblings and friends. Be specific.

_____

_____

_____

_____

_____

_____

_____

_____

Study No. 6, "Beauty and the Feast"

22. In Esther's life, we can see the beauty of obedience, trusting the authorities over us, discretion, respectful appeal, patience, courage, understanding of the character of others, and the wise use of the opportunities, position, and talents that God grants us. We also see the examples of Ahasuerus, Mordecai, and Haman. What can you learn from the lives of each of these men? What qualities can you emulate? What qualities will you avoid, with the Holy Spirit's help?

_____

_____

_____

_____

_____

_____

_____

Study No. 7, "Beauty on the Move"

1–9. Instead of studying the life of Sarah, study Abraham's life. Answer each of the questions as they relate to Abraham.

Study No. 9, "Beauty and the Fool"

39. In what similar ways can you show discretion in your own life? What can you also learn from David's example of discretion? Think about relationships with siblings, parents, friends, and neighbors. List specific actions you will take.

_____

_____

_____

_____

_____

_____

40. Review the attitudes and actions of both Nabal and David. What weaknesses do you see? What strengths? What similar weaknesses do you see in your own life? Apply what you have learned from this study to your own life. In what areas do you need to change? What specific actions, with God's help, can you take in obedience to His Holy Spirit's leading?

_____

_____

_____

_____

_____

_____

Study No. 10, "Beauty in the Gates"

12. Reread the entire book of Ruth, noting Boaz's words and actions. What can you learn from his example?

_____

_____

_____

_____

_____

_____

"Beauty in Review"

2. Skip this question.

3. Is God calling you to change in your attitudes and actions toward young women? After seeking the guidance of God and your parents, outline a specific plan to help you become more mature and obedient in your relationships with young women.

_____

_____

_____

_____

_____